EUROPE
in the
MIDDLE AGES

Contents

Things Fall Apart

Roads Lead to Rome You may have heard the expression "All roads lead to Rome." During the glory days of the Roman Empire, that saying was true. Rome was the center of the empire, and roads from all over Europe led there.

These roads allowed governors and judges to carry Roman ideas about law to the outlying regions of the empire. Messengers also traveled these roads, carrying instructions from the Roman emperor to the Roman governors. Roads allowed goods and taxes to travel from the outlying regions into Rome, too. These goods and taxes kept the powerful Roman Empire running. More important, perhaps, was that Roman soldiers used the roads to enforce the law and put down any rebellions or attacks on the empire.

The roads helped hold the Roman Empire together, but they also played a role in its eventual decline, for the Roman army was not the only army that could use these roads. The same roads that carried the Roman army out of Rome made it easier for outside invaders to march into the city. Beginning around A.D. 200, there were a number of non-Roman tribes that wanted to do just that.

At that time, Rome was still a vast and powerful empire, but it was facing some serious problems. Powerful Roman generals had been fighting each other. Each general wanted to gain enough power to become emperor. This was terrible for the health of the empire. A main purpose of the Roman government was to provide law and order so that people could conduct business and live in safety.

At its height the Roman Empire covered parts of Europe, Africa, and Asia.

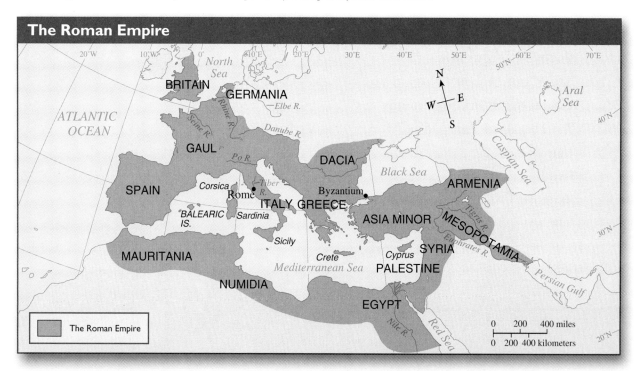

However, the wars between the generals undermined Roman law and order and interrupted business, trade, and government.

During these wars, so much money was spent on armies that Rome had less money to maintain roads and buildings. With poorer roads, trade decreased, and some of the people who had depended on trade to earn a living went out of business.

The Roman Empire grew weak enough in the 200s and 300s that it began to attract the attention of various tribes that lived on the fringes of the empire or outside its boundaries. Rome had conquered some of these tribes and had sent armies to guard the borders against others.

The Romans, who spoke Greek and Latin, looked down on these people and labeled them "barbarians." *Barbarian* was a Greek word for someone who spoke no Greek. The Romans dismissed non-Greek- and non-Latin-speaking barbarians as primitive, uncultured, and vastly inferior.

This was a classic example of something that happens all the time in history. However, many of the barbarian tribes were not uncivilized. Many tribes had skilled metalworkers who created beautiful jewelry and coins. Their languages belonged to a German language family rather than to Latin.

People on the Move

The Romans lumped a number of tribes into the barbarian category, including the Angles, the Saxons, the Huns, the Vandals, the Goths, the Ostrogoths, and the Visigoths. Several of these tribes were Germanic tribes who lived in northern Europe. The Angles and the Saxons lived in what is now Denmark and northern Germany. They eventually drove the Romans out of England. The Goths and Vandals attacked and eventually sacked the city of Rome itself. The Vandals caused so much destruction that, even today, we still use the word *vandalism* to describe acts of destruction.

However, the barbarians who left the longest memory of fear and destruction were not Germanic tribes. They were a nomadic people from central Asia called the Huns. The Huns lived on the steppes, a flat, grassy, treeless area that stretches for thousands of miles in what is now Ukraine, southern Russia, and Kazakhstan.

The Huns raised sheep, cattle, and horses on the steppes. As the seasons changed and the available grasses dried up, the tribes moved in search of new grazing lands for their livestock.

The Huns were amazing horsemen and experts with bows and arrows. They learned to ride horses as children, at the same time they learned to walk. So good was their horsemanship that one Roman historian described the Huns this way: "They are unable to put their feet on the ground. They live and sleep on their horses."

In the 300s the Huns, tired of trying to maintain themselves on the steppes, began to move westward across Europe. Due to their skill in warfare and their excellent horsemanship, the Huns easily conquered other tribes and moved onto their land.

Attila the Hun

Mysterious and terrorizing, the savage Huns struck fear into Romans and other tribes alike. But the most feared and notorious of all barbarians was Attila the Hun. For about ten years, Attila and his brother Bleda shared the throne as rulers of the Huns. But Attila wanted to rule alone—so badly that he killed his brother and became the sole king and leader of the Huns.

Attila became known as a brilliant but cruel general. He led the Huns westward, conquering other tribes and leaving devastation in his wake. The Huns crossed the Danube River and crushed a Roman army in eastern Europe. Then they invaded what is present-day France. At one point a Roman army combined with another barbarian tribe, the Visigoths, to defeat the Huns in a bloody battle in Gaul (present-day France). But that didn't stop Attila. It was to be his only defeat.

Next, Attila turned his attention on Rome itself. In 452 he blazed a path of destruction across northern Italy. In hopes of saving Rome, Pope Leo I, the bishop of Rome, rode out to meet with the feared Hun general. Most Romans thought that was the last they would see of Pope Leo. But in a dramatic face-to-face meeting, Attila thought he saw a halo around the pope's head. The cruel conqueror who feared no army was afraid of one man who seemed to have a power Attila knew nothing about. He decided to spare Rome. Soon after this meeting, Attila became sick and died. Without their leader and weakened by disease, the Huns retreated into eastern Europe.

The End of the Roman Empire

You may have heard the expression "Rome wasn't built in a day." It means that it takes a long time to accomplish a big task. It took hundreds of years before the Roman Empire reached its peak, and then it lasted for hundreds of years. At one point the Roman Empire was split into two parts—the Western Roman Empire centered in Rome and the Eastern Roman Empire ruled from Constantinople.

Finally, in 476, a German king called Odoacer (oh doh AY ser) attacked Rome and killed the emperor. Since no new emperor was named, the date 476 is accepted as the official end of the Western Roman Empire. The Eastern Roman Empire, which was not conquered, lasted for almost another thousand years.

In the next several lessons, you will read about a different way of life and government that came about in western Europe.

This painting shows Pope Leo on the left, protected by angels, meeting Attila who is on the black horse in the center.

Life as Usual Today, we say that the Middle Ages began in 476, when the western half of the Roman Empire collapsed. However, to the people of the time, especially those who lived outside of Rome in areas that are now part of France, Germany, or northern Italy, there wasn't any difference between life in 475 and 480.

Even though the Roman government ceased to exist, day-to-day life went on as before for most people. Many people probably did not even hear about the barbarians or the fall of Rome. And even in areas where the barbarians took over, many aspects of life remained more or less unchanged. Many of the barbarian tribes respected Roman ways, so the language and the relative positions of different types of people in society remained the same. Religions, customs, and laws did not change all of a sudden. People kept doing the things they had always done. Most people did not really care whether a Roman or a Germanic leader ruled the region they lived in, so long as law and order were preserved and they could feed themselves and their families.

Gradual Change

Over time, however, things did begin to change. Many roads and aqueducts built by the Romans to carry people, goods, and water began to fall apart. Although there were many local governments, there was now no central government with

money to fix the roads. Even if a ruler in one region decided to repair the roads that crossed his land, there was no guarantee that the roads in the next region would be any better.

Over a long time, trade dried up. During the time of the Roman Empire, there had been lively trade among the outposts in Europe and northern Africa, as well as the eastern Mediterranean regions. Those networks gradually stopped working, and around 600, it was nearly impossible to sell Europe's goods to northern Africa or to the eastern Mediterranean.

The Romans built well. This aqueduct still stands over the River Gare in France.

With the decline of trade, cities also began to shrink. Merchants who had depended on trade no longer had much to sell. The governors who had once carried out Roman laws were gone. Without stores and government offices, there were fewer places to work in the cities. Some cities got smaller. Others just disappeared entirely.

Most people survived by farming or soldiering. With no government to pay for big public buildings or ships, artisans couldn't practice their skills. Today, we have many books that explain how to do different things. In those times, when few people could read or write, skills were passed from a skilled worker to a younger worker. When the skills were no longer used and passed on, people simply forgot how to do things. People forgot how to build domes and large ships because there was simply no use for these things during this time.

The Dark Ages

Because people forgot some things that were known by the Greeks and Romans, this period from about 500 to 800 was once called the Dark Ages. You may wonder why the terms *barbarian* and *Dark Ages* were ever introduced.

There was a rivalry between the Middle Ages and the period that followed—the Renaissance. Many Renaissance scholars tended to look down on the Middle Ages and dismiss them as dark ages when there was no learning. Because many modern people admired the artists and scholars of the Renaissance, people tended to accept what the Renaissance writers said about the Middle Ages.

Today, historians present a more balanced view, admitting the shortcomings of the Middle Ages but also noting its strengths. It is true that some valuable skills were forgotten during this time. Since travel was difficult and potentially dangerous, most people tended to stay in their own areas. The Middle Ages also had its fair share of violence. However, today historians agree that the Middle Ages were probably not any more violent than the time of the Roman Empire or the Renaissance. Modern historians see these years as a time of change and growth, contributing to the rise of Western civilization in many ways.

Spreading Out

The history of western Europe in this period may seem very distant. But in the years following the fall of Rome, nations that would play important roles in European history were being created.

Remember the destructive Visigoths who sacked Rome? They continued to move westward, into present-day France. Then they crossed the Pyrenees mountains and moved into Spain and Portugal, where they settled into a life of farming. Another related tribe, the Ostrogoths, moved into central Europe, the present-day Czech Republic and Hungary. The Huns were absorbed by other ethnic groups. The Angles and Saxons moved across the sea to England, whose name comes from the Angles—"Angle-land."

History is a little like making a cake. Many ingredients go into it—and something very different comes out. In these years the tribes that brought down the Roman Empire began the process of creating a new and different Europe.

The Bishop of Rome Although the city of Rome was much smaller after the fall of the Roman Empire, it was still a city. People living in the city still needed food and other supplies.

It is very difficult for people who live in cities to grow the food they need. Food has to come from farming areas outside the city. However, now there was no one to take charge and arrange for these kinds of supplies to be brought into Rome. Who would perform those duties now?

Remember when Attila the Hun almost attacked Rome? The person who talked him out of doing that was Leo. He was the bishop of Rome. There was still an emperor at that time, but the power of the emperor was fading fast. The power of Rome's bishop, however, was growing.

The Victors Convert

The Germanic tribes had conquered the Roman lands. And yet, in a sense, these tribes had been conquered too, though not by the Roman army. The Germanic tribes were conquered by the Roman church. Remember that Rome was a Christian empire by 476. Nearly all the tribes who took Rome's lands eventually became Christians themselves. They took on both the religion and the customs of Rome.

In addition, many of them began to speak the language of Rome. That is why French, Italian, and Spanish, the languages spoken in southern Europe today, are called Romance languages. They are more closely related to the Latin language of Rome than they are to the Germanic languages of the people who conquered Rome.

Even though newcomers had conquered Rome, they admired what it stood for. It had been the center of the most powerful empire of their world for hundreds of years. Many Roman laws and customs, the Latin language, and

During a time of disease and famine, Pope Gregory I, the bishop of Rome, leads a procession to pray at St. Peter's Basilica.

the Roman religion were respected and preserved by these victorious invaders.

When there was no longer an emperor, the bishop of Rome became the most important official in the city. Pope Leo believed that his power as bishop of Rome extended far beyond the city of Rome itself. Leo said the bishop of Rome was the most important official in the Christian Church. He felt that his power extended over all other churches throughout the lands of the Roman Empire and beyond.

What reasoning did Leo use to support his claim to power? He claimed that the power of the bishop of Rome came from Jesus himself, through Saint Peter. Leo said that Jesus had chosen Peter, one of his followers, to be the head of the church after the death of Jesus. According to Christian belief, Peter left Jerusalem after Jesus was crucified and went to Rome. Leo and his supporters believed that Peter became the first bishop of Rome and that all the bishops of Rome after him were heirs to his position as head of the Christian Church.

Using this argument, Leo and other bishops of Rome who followed him claimed that the bishop of Rome was the *papa*, or father, of the Christian Church. The former Western Roman Empire was broken up into many smaller kingdoms and territories. As leader of the Church in all these regions, however, the bishop of Rome claimed power throughout Europe. Do you know what the bishop of Rome is also called today? If you said *pope*, you are right.

The Eastern Empire

There was just one problem with this idea, or, rather, there were four problems. You see, there were four other bishops who also viewed themselves as leaders of the

Christian Church. These were the bishops of Constantinople, Alexandria, Antioch, and Jerusalem. These cities were all located in the Eastern Roman Empire.

Remember how the Roman Empire was divided into two parts? One part was the Western Roman Empire, centered around Rome. The other part was the Eastern Roman Empire, also known as the Byzantine Empire. The Emperor Constantine, the first Christian emperor of the Roman Empire, in

the early 300s built a new capital at the ancient Greek city of Byzantium. He named this new capital Constantinople. While the Western Empire was weakened by internal problems and eventually destroyed by invaders, the Eastern Empire survived.

However, the Eastern Empire was much less Roman than the parts of the empire that had been conquered by the Germanic tribes. The eastern part of the empire was more Greek than Roman. Most of its people did not speak Latin or languages that were influenced by Latin. Do you think the bishops of Alexandria, Antioch, and Jerusalem would be more influenced by the bishop of Constantinople or the bishop of Rome?

If you said Constantinople, you were right. Over time the differences between the Christians in what had once been the western part of the empire and the Christians in the eastern part of the empire got stronger. There

Hagia Sophia, the Church of the Holy Wisdom, was built in the sixth century in Constantinople as the main cathedral for the Eastern Empire.

Over the centuries they had developed a very different tradition of governing the Church and its religious customs. They did, however, accept the belief that the bishop of Rome was the heir of Saint Peter.

During this time, the bishop of Rome took on more power and demanded that the eastern bishops accept his authority. In 1054 the differences came to a head between the bishops of Rome and Constantinople. After some major disagreements, the two churches separated.

had always been some differences, of course. Even though both groups were Christians, they spoke different languages and had different cultures. More and more disagreements sprang up between the two groups. Some of these disagreements may seem trivial today, but they were passionately debated in the Middle Ages. For example, Christians in the former Western Empire used flat bread made without yeast in their holy ceremonies. Christians in the Eastern Empire used bread made with yeast in their holy ceremonies.

More important than such issues was the larger issue of who was in charge of the Church. Bishops in the Eastern Empire did not like accepting the rule of the bishop of Rome as the final word on all Church matters. They were used to ruling in a more cooperative manner, in which each bishop had a vote.

Two Separate Churches

Christian bishops in the Eastern Empire, including Bulgarians, Serbs, Russians, Syrians, and Egyptians, chose to join with the bishop of Constantinople. People on both sides of this argument expected that the division between the two parts of the Church was just temporary.

Over time, however, the two sides did not get back together. In fact, they found more reasons to disagree. Today, the church that is headed by the bishop of Rome (the pope) is known as the Roman Catholic Church. The church in the region that was ruled by Constantinople (now Istanbul, Turkey) is generally known as the Eastern Orthodox Church. In the rest of this unit, we will study mostly the lands of the Western Church.

4 Prayer and Work

Saint Benedict of Nursia About the time of the fall of the Western Roman Empire, a boy named Bennet was born in the mountain village of Nursia, northeast of Rome. He was a serious child who thought a lot about right and wrong. He was described as having "the mind of an old man" in a young man's body.

Bennet's parents sent him to Rome to study, but he was upset by the sinfulness he saw around him. Bennet was shocked by the lying, cheating, and dishonesty he saw in the city. He left Rome and decided to live as a monk, devoting himself to a religious life. At that time there were many monks in Asia, but there were very few of them in Europe.

The European monks who did exist lived isolated from the world as hermits, denying themselves the comforts of life for religious reasons. Many of them did things that were harsh and painful to themselves, like going without food or living in a cave for years on end. That is what Bennet did at first. He spent three years living in a cave.

Benedict's good works and holiness made him one of the important saints of the Catholic Church.

Eventually, Bennet, now called Benedict, decided that it was not enough to pray in a cave. He believed that monks should serve God and people. Benedict's years in a cave spread his fame as a holy man. A group of rich monks invited him to become the leader of a **monastery**. Benedict accepted, but things did not go very well. When Benedict tried to get them to serve God by helping other people, they refused. It got so bad that the other monks even tried to poison Benedict.

Benedict saw that to realize his bold new ideas he would have to start his own

> **vocabulary**
> **monastery a community of monks**

monastery. He moved to the town of Monte Cassino and wrote a book that is known today as *The Rule of Saint Benedict*. This book contained a list of rules to be enforced in the monastery. Instead of urging people to seek holiness through pain or fasting—going without food and water—Benedict urged monks to find God in ordinary, simple, and useful work. Work was balanced with prayer and reading, sleeping, and eating. He also emphasized the importance of working with and getting along with everyone in the monastery, especially those who were annoying or difficult to get along with. He felt that finding the ability to see Christ in everyone was the path to God.

Monte Cassino was destroyed during World War II and has been rebuilt.

Self-Sufficient and Hard-Working

Monte Cassino was a successful monastery, and Benedict's fame spread. Soon other monasteries were created to follow his rules.

Monasteries following Saint Benedict's rules were called Benedictine monasteries. These monasteries tried to be self-sufficient. That means that the monks grew and made almost everything they needed themselves. They had gardens in which they raised their own vegetables. They kept chickens and goats to provide eggs and milk that they used to make cheese. They also baked all their own bread, sewed their own clothing, brewed beers, and made wines.

Does it seem strange that deeply religious people made beer and wine to drink? This is a good example of how customs change over time. In the Middle Ages almost everyone drank small amounts of beer every day. Beer was considered a healthy drink because of the grains used to make it. There was just one meal a day, with a cold snack in the evening. Meals consisted of bread with eggs, cheese, or fish. The monks ate at assigned places. There was no conversation during the meals, but one monk read aloud from the Scriptures or a religious book.

Benedict also required monks to follow a shared schedule. When the bell rang for prayer, everyone in the monastery stopped whatever he was doing and went to the chapel.

A day in the monastery was divided into three general work periods. Monks spent about six hours in prayer, six hours doing manual work such as gardening, cooking, or sewing. And around four hours were spent in studying and writing. Monks slept seven to eight hours a night. Saint Benedict's rules are interesting to read in today's busy times. Monks worked hard and were productive, but they also lived healthy, balanced lives.

The **abbot** made the rules in the monastery, and all monks had to obey him. Monks were required to show hospitality to all guests, whether invited or not, and to treat all the monastery's possessions—whether gardening tools or precious altar pieces—with care and reverence.

Missionaries, Hospitals, Schools, and Libraries

The Rule of Saint Benedict had a great influence not only on Benedictine monasteries but also on other types of monasteries that developed later on, as well as on **convents**. Altogether these religious institutions had a great impact on the history of Europe.

Monasteries took on the role of supplying missionaries to bring Christianity to people who followed older non-Christian religions. Saint Benedict himself spread Christianity in the area around Monte Cassino. One of the most famous missionaries was Saint Patrick, who brought the Christian religion to Ireland. Saint Augustine, another famous missionary, brought Christianity to the Anglo-Saxons of Britain. Saint Boniface converted many of the tribes in what is now Germany.

Saint Benedict also saw the role of the monastery as helping the poor. During this time, government provided no help for poor people. What help was provided came from the Church, from priests, monks, and nuns who saw caring for the poor as their Christian duty.

Monks and nuns also ran hospitals for the sick who were too poor to hire their own doctors, and schools for children training to become monks and nuns.

One of the most important things that monasteries and convents did for Europe was to set up libraries. In the early Middle Ages,

books were rare and expensive. Every book that existed had been written or copied by hand! Although there were important Islamic libraries in Asia and Africa, in Europe almost all the libraries that existed were in monasteries.

Most people in Europe had little need for reading. Some went their whole lives without ever seeing a book. Information was passed along several ways. Most people learned by watching and doing. Children would watch their parents make things, take care of animals, and farm. Once they learned to do these things, they would get married, have children, and pass these skills on to their children. For more skilled crafts, such as shoemaking, barrel making, and others, young men would work alongside master craftspersons and learn the craft.

Few people learned how to do things from reading books. People learned about the Bible from listening to a priest, monk, or nun. For the most part, the only people who knew how to read were priests, monks, and nuns. There was no mystery to this. Practically the only schools that existed were religious schools. And most of the students there were in training for a religious career.

Reading was an important activity in many monasteries and convents, but few people sat and read silently to themselves. Most of the time one person would read aloud to a group. If people wanted to make an oath, it was considered more important to say it out loud than to write it down and sign it. The ability to read and write was so unusual and so highly valued that many people believed that it was a special gift from God to the servants of God. Even those of us who read well today would have had trouble reading manuscripts from the early Middle Ages, though. Practically all of them were written in Latin, and the writing was hard to follow.

Even after the fall of the Roman Empire, the Latin language that had been used in the empire remained the official written language in Europe. Any document that had religious, legal, or scholarly significance was written in Latin.

In the early Middle Ages (and also in ancient Rome), reading was difficult because words were not separated or punctuated.

NOWONDERITWASHARDFORME
DIEVALPEOPLETOREADTHEYDIDNOT
HAVECOMMASPERIODSORSPACES
BETWEENWORDS

Imagine reading a whole book that way! That was why around the year 800 monks began to put spaces between words, mark the end of sentences, and invent the small letters we use today.

Monks worked to copy the texts of books that did exist. Most of the books they copied were longer than the book you are reading now. Think of how long it would take you to copy every word in this book by hand. Monks didn't just copy the words, either. They also decorated the important first letters and borders of their manuscripts. Maybe you can see now why books were so rare and expensive. Think of how long it would have taken to make one! Today, these handwritten books from the Middle Ages are considered valuable works of art.

Monasteries still exist in the modern world, and monks and nuns continue the work they have done for more than a thousand years. Today, however, there are thousands of schools, universities, hospitals, and libraries all over the world. That is why it may be hard to imagine how important the work of the Benedictine monasteries was to the lives of Europeans. For many centuries, the monks and nuns were the teachers, writers, librarians, book publishers, doctors, and nurses for all of Europe.

Knowledge was kept alive by monks who would spend enormous amounts of time copying books for monastery libraries.

A Head Above the Others Monks and monasteries spread Christianity through much of what was Europe. In the late 700s, however, one man would come along who was not a monk but who would do more than any other person to spread Christianity and strengthen the Western Church.

That man was Charles, the king of the Franks. The Franks were a tribe that lived along the Rhine River in present-day Germany. Charles was not just the king. He might have been the tallest man in his kingdom. Charles was 6 feet 3 1/2 inches tall. (We know that because his bones have been measured.) Even by today's standards, that is tall. But in the 700s, when Europeans were much shorter than people in Europe or the United States today, it was really tall. Charles towered about a head above everyone else.

Charles was not only tall but was healthy and energetic as well. He followed health advice you've probably heard all your life! He ate healthy foods, exercised every day (he loved to swim), and got plenty of rest (he took a nap every day). He was a hard worker, too. He started having meetings the minute he got out of bed, before he had finished dressing. His advisors would come into his bedroom and ask him questions.

Charles's greatest talent was organizing and managing people. He knew how to inspire armies to fight, and he also knew how to move them quickly from one place to another. This was an important skill for a leader in a time when there were no reliable maps. He didn't give up, either. Once he started something, he finished it and he expected the same of his men.

Charles enjoyed being king. Like most rulers, he enjoyed the power of ruling. But unlike some kings, he had goals beyond gaining power for himself. He wanted to spread Christianity, and he wanted to foster learning and culture. These noble goals and Charles's ability to make them happen

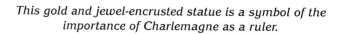

This gold and jewel-encrusted statue is a symbol of the importance of Charlemagne as a ruler.

combined to make him one of the greatest rulers Europe had ever known. Charles became so great that "great" became part of his name. By the time he died, people were calling him *Charlemagne* (SHAHR luh mayn), which means Charles the Great, and that is what historians today call him.

To the Rescue

The Frankish army was an impressive sight. Strong and disciplined, they wore leather vests and light armor. Their most important weapons were their swords, and Frankish soldiers treated their swords with care. Many of them had scabbards, a case for a sword, decorated with silver, gold, and even jewels.

The Frankish army was very successful in battle. These strong soldiers with their glittering weapons conquered much of the territory that had once been part of the Western Roman Empire. The Muslims (called Moors by Europeans) controlled central Spain, but Charlemagne took parts of northern Spain, as well as most of what is now France, Germany, Switzerland, Holland, Belgium, and Luxembourg and united them into a Frankish empire. He also took northern Italy from the Lombards, a Germanic tribe.

In an earlier lesson you read about how the bishop of Rome, also known as the pope, was trying to exert more leadership after the fall of the Western Roman Empire and that the bishops of Constantinople, Alexandria, Antioch, and Jerusalem didn't like that very much. But Pope Leo III had enemies closer to home. Powerful princes from the lands around Rome grew jealous of the Church's wealth and power. The pope's enemies actually attacked him as he was walking through the streets of Rome! They pushed him to the ground, pulled off his robes, and beat him up. He woke up covered with cuts and bruises.

The pope fled from Rome and appealed to Charlemagne for help. Charlemagne did not let the pope down. He sent an army to escort the pope back to Rome, where his soldiers punished the pope's enemies.

The following year, Charlemagne went to Rome for two purposes. He wanted to make sure the pope was safe from any more attacks, and he wanted to celebrate Christmas with the pope. It was A.D. 800, the beginning of a new century, a special year, and Charlemagne wanted to celebrate it with the pope in St. Peter's Church.

Emperor of the Romans

The celebration proved to be much more special than Charlemagne had dreamed possible. According to Charlemagne's biographer Einhard, Charlemagne prepared for a traditional Christmas mass. He planned to wear his usual Frankish clothing, but the pope asked him to wear a Roman toga and sandals instead. Out of respect for the pope, Charlemagne agreed. When he arrived at the cathedral, he found it packed with people from all over his kingdom. Romans, Franks, Bavarians, Greeks, Lombards, and Anglo-Saxons were gathered there. Even Charlemagne's children were there.

When Charlemagne reached the front of the cathedral, he knelt in prayer. After a long time he stood up, and the pope placed a crown on Charlemagne's head. The people in the Church broke out in a cheer. "Long life and victory to Charles Augustus, crowned by God, great and peaceful emperor of the Romans," they cried.

Reading this today, it is hard to believe that Charlemagne was totally surprised by being crowned by the pope. But that's the story that has come down through the ages.

The crowning of Charlemagne as emperor accomplished three things. It gave the Romans an emperor for the first time since 476, it gave Charlemagne the blessing of the pope, and it established that Charlemagne agreed that the pope had the power to crown an emperor.

A Great Ruler

Charlemagne expanded his kingdom through warfare. However, what made him great wasn't what he did on the battlefield but was what he did with his kingdom after he won it.

Charlemagne built a beautiful capital city, Aachen (AH ken), in what is now northwestern Germany. He built a palace and a chapel. He also had a great library. He even built a huge swimming pool out of marble. The pool was filled with water from natural hot springs and was big enough for 100 people to swim in at once. He started a school in his palace and allowed the sons of poor people to attend as well as the children of nobles. Charlemagne believed that women should be educated as well as men, an unusual view for his time. He even tried to provide free education to all his subjects.

Charlemagne was a good manager in times of peace as well as in war. He improved communication and management throughout his empire. He sent teams of ambassadors chosen for their good character to enforce laws and solve conflicts in the kingdom. Like the Romans, he built roads and bridges to make trade and travel easier.

When Charlemagne first began conquering the Saxons and other tribes, he tried to force them to become Christians. At first his rule was very harsh. People who would not convert to Christianity were killed. Later in his life, however, Charlemagne realized that force was not the best way to win souls. By the 790s he allowed his conquered subjects to make their own choices about Christianity. He also rewrote many laws to make them fairer.

In 800, Pope Leo III crowned Charlemagne emperor of the Romans.

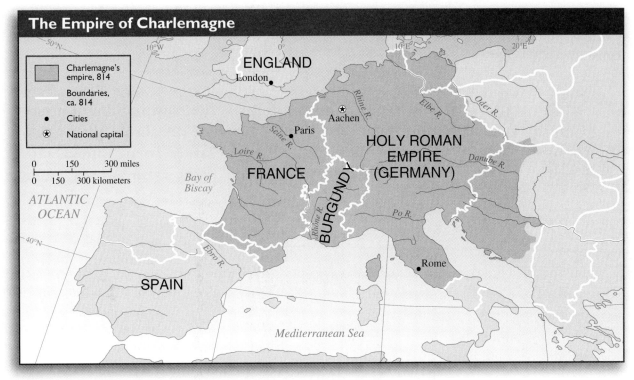

The Empire of Charlemagne

Charlemagne's empire, 814
Boundaries, ca. 814
• Cities
★ National capital

0   150   300 miles
0   150   300 kilometers

ENGLAND
London
ATLANTIC OCEAN
Bay of Biscay
Seine R.
Paris
Aachen ★
Rhine R.
Loire R.
FRANCE
BURGUNDY
Rhone R.
Ebro R.
SPAIN
HOLY ROMAN EMPIRE (GERMANY)
Elbe R.
Oder R.
Danube R.
Po R.
Rome
Mediterranean Sea

Charlemagne ruled a vast area that included many different people.

Charlemagne died in 814. None of the rulers who followed had his gift for leadership. The empire that Charlemagne created did not last. However, it set a new standard for learning and management. It brought the people of many tribes together and helped form some of the modern countries of Europe.

The Franks originally spoke an early form of German. By the time of Charlemagne's death, however, many Franks were speaking a new language that was influenced by Latin. This language became known (to English speakers) as French and the country where it is spoken as France. Over the next 200 or 300 years, the French-speaking part of Charlemagne's empire broke away to form the kingdom of France.

The Holy Roman Empire

Charlemagne's empire continued in various forms for centuries. Part of it was expanding toward the east. It still included Rome, however, and there was a strong alliance between the pope and the rulers of this German-speaking empire.

In the 1200s the Hapsburg family took power over this German empire. It was at this point that it became known as the Holy Roman Empire, having been blessed by the pope. This empire now included the areas that are today Germany, Holland, Belgium, Switzerland, Luxembourg, Austria, the Czech Republic, western Poland, northern Italy, and eastern France. It stretched roughly from the North Sea and Baltic Sea in the north to the Mediterranean in the south and from the Rhone River in the west to beyond the Oder River in the east.

A **New Society** Who do you think is the most important person in your town? In every society there are certain people who are more important and more powerful than others. In the United States today, power and importance often come with money, some special abilities, or elected office.

In the Middle Ages there were no political elections and few offices that one could get by having special abilities. Money didn't make you important in the same way it can today. The important people in the Middle Ages were those who controlled land, especially the kings and the lords and knights who fought for the kings.

With the end of the Roman Empire, everyday life for most people continued much the same. But the nobles—the important people of the Roman Empire—lost some power. Powerful soldiers who conquered Germanic tribes were awarded more power. These warriors became the new nobility of a new society that continued for more than a thousand years. The system that developed around these new leaders is usually called **feudalism**.

A Special System

Feudalism appeared first in France after Charlemagne's time, and later it spread to some other medieval kingdoms. It arose because kings needed warriors to fight for them and therefore made deals with powerful fighters. The fighter (or lord, as he was now known) would become the king's **vassal.** The king would give him a large amount of land, called a **fief,** and each would make certain promises to the other. The vassal would swear to fight

loyally for the king; the king pledged to protect and be loyal to the vassal.

Feudal government was not like modern government. During the Middle Ages there were no

vocabulary
feudalism a system of government in which land is exchanged for loyalty and services
vassal a person who receives land from a ruler and in return promises aid
fief a plot of land exchanged for loyalty to a ruler

The feudal system was based on the relationship between the lord, who could be the king, and his vassals.

nations in the modern sense—no central governments with bureaus, branches, and departments. There were only networks of lords and vassals under the supervision of a king. However, the oaths that vassals swore held these networks together. The interlocking links between vassals and lords encouraged people to think of themselves as part of a larger whole. Eventually, some of these networks of lords and vassals evolved into modern European nations.

A feudal agreement was meant to be a long-term arrangement. In the Middle Ages it was arranged by kings and priests and sealed in a church. The ceremony in which a man became a vassal was called an act of homage (HAHM ihj). *Homage* is the French word for "honor" or "respect." Let's time-travel back to the Middle Ages and watch as a medieval lord pays homage to a king.

"Kiss of Peace"

Imagine we are in a cathedral lit by hundreds of flickering candles. There are beautiful windows of stained glass and paintings and sculptures. The altar is made of beautifully carved wood. Sitting in the cathedral are all the great lords of the kingdom and their families dressed in their finest robes and jewels. At the front stands the king, waiting to receive his vassal.

A lord walks slowly down the center aisle of the cathedral. When he reaches the king, he falls to his knees and recites an oath that might have sounded something like this:

> Lord, I become your man. From this day forth, I will love what you love and loathe what you loathe, and never by word or deed will I do anything that will grieve you.

Then, the king raises the kneeling man to his feet and announces that he was bestowing land upon the lord in exchange for an eternal vow of loyalty and other services. The king kisses his new vassal on the cheek in a "kiss of peace."

What made feudalism work was that it was not limited to the king and his lords. The king's lords would divide up part of their land and grant fiefs to vassals of their own. The king's vassal might rule a large area called a duchy or a county. That made his title duke or count. The dukes and counts would grant portions of their to land lesser lords and to other soldiers called **knights**.

Feudal Government

Feudal loyalties usually preserved law and order within a kingdom, but there were few laws across kingdoms. Individual lords made their own laws and enforced them in their own fiefs. The one law that extended across Europe was the sacred oath of loyalty that a vassal took. If a vassal failed to serve his lord or betrayed his lord, he became an outlaw, shunned and persecuted by other lords.

vocabulary
knight a military servant of a feudal king or other superior

Over the years these titles and arrangements became hereditary—they were handed down from father to son. The families who held fiefs became the nobility of central and western Europe in the Middle Ages. As nobles they had special privileges that other people did not have. In the next several lessons, you will read how feudalism provided a way for people to make a living and how it also created its own culture of knights, battles, and honor that is still remembered today.

7 To the Manor Born

A **Self-sufficient Village** You might be wondering what happened to the land that the vassals received from their lords. You probably know enough about dukes and counts and other nobles to know that they weren't likely to be out milking cows and planting crops.

On the other hand there were plenty of people living during the Middle Ages who needed to eat but who did not receive fiefs from a king.

In much of northern Europe, each lord lived in a castle or **manor** house, surrounded by the land on which food was grown and where the people who worked in the fields lived. The manor estate was a lot like a village. Nearly everything that people needed was grown or made there. In addition to their food, people who lived on the estate made their own soap, candles, furniture, leather, tools, and cloth. Most of the people who lived on the estate farmed, but there were a few specialists, like blacksmiths who made things out of metal.

In addition to the manor house and cottages of people who lived on the estate, you would probably also find a church building on a manor estate. Sunday worship, baptisms, weddings, and funerals were conducted there. Next to the church there would probably be a graveyard where people from the estate were buried when they died.

Exchanging Labor for Land

The lord of the manor allowed **serfs**, farmers who were bound to the lord's land, to use his land. The serfs grew food on the land, raised animals that grazed on the land, and used the wood from the forests. The lord also provided a mill to grind the grain grown on the manor, large community ovens for baking the grain into bread, costly equipment like plows and wagons, and teams of oxen to pull the plows and wagons.

vocabulary

manor the estate over which a lord had control; also the lord's house on an estate

serf a farmworker who was bound to live and labor on his lord's land

Manor

Pasture

Workshop

Serfs' Houses

Third Field

Barn

The lord of the manor had other responsibilities. The lord provided the serfs with law and order and protection. The lord could spare a serf for stealing if he felt like it. Or he could punish him severely. The lord was limited in these matters by the law of the church. In other words, he could not punish or kill someone without a reason.

The lord also protected the people who lived on the manor. If an enemy were to attack, the lord's army would protect his people. The lord did not provide these important services without getting a lot from the serfs in return. The serfs had to spend about three days a week working in the fields that grew food for the lord of the manor and his household. During certain times of the year, like the planting and the harvesting seasons, the amount of work required could be increased.

A manor house, a church, and a mill were all part of a typical village of the Middle Ages.

Serfs also had to give part of everything they grew for themselves to the lord of the manor. They had to give the lord a portion of all the milk they got from their goats and cows and of the eggs they got from their chickens. If they collected firewood in the forest, they had to give some of it to him, and if they used the lord's mill to grind their grain into flour, they had to give the lord some of that as well.

In addition, the serfs had to provide other services to the lord. For example, the serfs had to keep the walls of the lord's manor repaired. If heavy barrels needed to be stacked or moved, the serfs had to do it. If war broke out, serfs had to help defend the lord's land. If the lord had guests, serfs might have work in the stables taking care of the extra horses or in the kitchen to help prepare the food. This meant the serfs had little time for their regular chores.

You might wonder why serfs would agree to give the lord so much. The answer is that they had little choice. In the Middle Ages, power determined who ruled. The lords had all the power. They had the weapons and the knowledge of how to rule. The times were violent, and no peasant family could survive without some lord's protection. The Church supported the feudal arrangements, so almost everybody went along with them. As you might guess, serfs did not have easy lives. They had to work very hard just to get enough to feed their families.

The Three-Field System

Despite all this hard work, there was not always enough food for all the people who worked the land and their families. The soil in England and the parts of Europe north of the Alps was rich, but the growing season was short and rainy. People had to make the most of what they had.

In the Middle Ages, people had little of the scientific knowledge we have today. But they did know something about farming. Working in the fields every day, people learned that if a field was farmed year after year, it lost its ability to grow healthy crops. They came up with a solution to that problem: the three-field system. In this system, all the cropland on an estate was divided into three parts. Each year, one part was planted in the spring, one part was planted in the fall, and one part was left fallow, or unplanted. Thus a particular field would be used differently in different years. One year it might be used to grow crops planted in the spring, like wheat and rye. The next year, it would be used to grow crops planted in the fall, like oats, barley, and beans. The third year the field would be left fallow. This gave the soil a chance to recover.

The three-field system allowed the soil to keep renewing itself. The crops that were planted in the spring used different nutrients than those that were planted in the fall.

A lord of the manor instructs the workers in his gardens. Note the differences in the clothing of the lord and the serfs.

The fields that were fallow had a chance to recover nutrients as old matter broke down and replenished the soil.

Cooperation Was the Key

People on a manor estate had to cooperate with one another. They lived closely together. They had to share pastureland. They had to cooperate about when to plant wheat and oats and when to leave fields fallow. People cooperated to create goods for trade. Certain things were not available on a European manor estate, like salt and iron, so everyone had to cooperate to trade for it.

Cooperation was essential to survival. It wasn't just voluntary. A smart lord took care of his serfs and tried to keep them happy. Yet the lord was always the boss. In the society of the Middle Ages, he was superior to the serfs—and no one questioned that.

The residents of the manor came together for special holidays. Christmas and Easter and many other religious holidays were celebrated together. The lord, his family, and serfs would attend church together. There would be a feast, games, and celebrations for holidays during the year. In this way, serfs and their lord formed a community that endured through the centuries of the Middle Ages.

Castles: Dream and Reality You've probably heard fairy tales about kings and queens and castles. There's always something magical going on in fairy tales. Wizards, witches, and fairy godmothers are likely to be hanging around the castle casting and breaking spells.

Castles are real, however, even if some of the characters in these stories are not. Even today you can see castles all over England, Spain, France, Germany, Portugal, and other parts of Europe. In this lesson you'll learn why people built castles and what it was like to live in one.

Castle Fortress

Castles were fortresses. Lords built castles to defend themselves and their manors against attacks. The forts were usually built on high ground. This way the defenders could look down on the attacking enemy. In the early Middle Ages, people built forts out of wood. A big ditch called a moat was built surrounding the wooden fence.

If you were attacking such a fort, what would you do? If you answered "Burn it!" you would have made a good general in the Middle Ages. Wooden castles were easy to build, but they provided no protection against flaming arrows.

Lords realized they needed to build castles out of stone to get any real protection from invaders. So that is what they did. It was certainly a lot more work. But by the year 1000 stone castles were spreading across Europe.

What did a stone castle look like? What was it like to live and fight in one? Read on and find out!

Castle Construction

Put yourself in the place of a lord in the Middle Ages. You need to build a castle. What's the first thing you're going to think about? If you answered "location," you get an "A" for good thinking.

A castle needed to be in a place that would be easy to defend. Ever wonder why so many castles are built on hilltops? A hilltop was easy to defend. Soldiers could see their enemies coming. The enemies had to get up the hill while soldiers looked on them from above. Castles had high watchtowers for spotting approaching enemies.

Most castles were surrounded by tall walls and a water-filled moat. Some castles had more than one moat and more than one wall. Drawbridges could be lowered or raised to create or remove a roadway over the moat. These extra walls and moats provided additional lines of defense. Some castles also had underground tunnels for moving soldiers between different parts of the castle. On top of the walls there would usually be walkways from which soldiers could fire arrows or dump boulders and hot oil down on the attacking enemy.

The center of the castle was called the keep. Some of the area in a castle's keep was open courtyard; other areas were covered to provide protected living and working space.

The keep was built to hold out for a long time against an enemy who surrounded the castle. In the keep there were stables, workshops, a large oven, and a kitchen.

There was a well for water and stalls for farm animals. There were storerooms where grains and other foods were kept as well. These stores were not unlimited, however. Many people—nobles, servants, and soldiers—lived inside a castle. Eventually, all the grain would be used up. The chickens would stop laying eggs, the cows would stop giving milk, and all the pigs would have been eaten. Still, people could survive behind a castle's walls for many months.

Castles in War

Castles were strong forts; but well-armed, patient attackers could take a castle. Attackers dug tunnels under the stone walls. Then they stuffed the tunnels with gunpowder and set them on fire, causing the walls to collapse.

Since castles were so strong, direct attack rarely worked. Most attackers relied on siege, or blockade, to win the battle. In a siege an attacking army would surround the castle so that no food, weapons, or supplies could reach the people inside. Castles were prepared for sieges. But after weeks they would use up their supplies. Only then would the attackers attempt to take the castle, since the defenders were weak from hunger.

Attackers used siege towers, tall wooden towers that rolled on wheels and could hold soldiers. These towers were rolled up to the castle walls. Soldiers inside the tower climbed up the tower and over the castle walls.

The battering ram was another method used by attackers. Many soldiers were required to hold up a huge log that was banged against the heavy, ironclad castle doors until the doors broke open. Battering down the door was difficult. Castle doors were strong. And the men holding up the battering ram were under constant attack from defenders high on the castle walls.

Attackers also shot flaming arrows into the keep. The walls may have been stone, but castles still had buildings made out of wood, plus hay in the stables, and other items that could catch fire.

Still, a castle was a strong fortress. A small army could hold out against a much larger force.

A castle in the Middle Ages was like a small city.

Sometimes, what decided the battle was action outside the castle. A lord under siege would try to get word to other vassals to come to his aid. An army surrounding the castle had to be prepared to fight both the castle troops and another army.

Life in a Castle

Castles were very expensive to build, but that doesn't mean that they were nice to live in. In fact, living in an early castle was more like living in a cave than in a mansion. Castles were usually cold, drafty, and dirty places.

Many people lived in the castle, but few of them had their own rooms or apartments. Most people lived and ate in the Great Hall, the largest inside room in the castle. In early castles the lord and lady might have had a bed in a corner of the hall. Everyone else slept on the floor, often piling any clothes they happened to have under and over themselves for warmth.

The Great Hall was also used for meals. Again, the lord and lady would probably have had chairs to sit in, but everyone else would have sat on long benches alongside tables. After everyone had eaten, the tables were put aside to provide room to sleep. Some early halls did not even have fireplaces. An open fire was built in a stone hearth in the center of the room. You can see why it was a lot like camping in a cave!

It was hard to keep these castles clean. Dogs were allowed to run free in the Great

A rich lord might hire a jester, also called a fool, to entertain his guests by telling funny stories.

Hall. There were no flush toilets, just closets built into the edges of walls. Wastes fell into pits or moats along the outside of the castle. Lords and ladies occasionally took baths and washed their hands, but servants did not have many chances to wash.

Over time, castles did become more comfortable, especially for the nobles who lived in them. Fireplaces were added. More people had beds and their own bedrooms. Cold stone walls were hung with tapestries or even paneled with wood to cut down on drafts.

The Great Hall was still a center of activity, though. Musical performers, storytellers, and jugglers entertained people while they ate and after dinner, especially during the winter when it got dark early and the only light in the castle might come from the fire in the Great Hall.

Castles were so well built that many still stand nearly a thousand years after they were built. Castle building changed along with weapons and warfare during the Middle Ages. During the early Middle Ages, foot soldiers used bows and arrows as their main weapons. You can see how thick castle walls would be a good defense against the bow and arrow. But toward the end of the Middle Ages, the use of cannons in battle made it easier to break down a castle's walls. The coming of the cannon brought the great age of the castle to an end.

A **Knight in Shining Armor** Close your eyes. Imagine a column of knights on horseback marching out across the drawbridge of a castle to fight a distant enemy. It's a bright sunny day, and the sunshine glints off their armor, creating a dazzling sight.

Mounted knights were important figures in the Middle Ages. In military terms an army of knights could turn the tide of any battle. And knights were also important figures influencing the songs and stories of the Middle Ages.

How did one become a knight? What was a knight's training like? What did knights do when they weren't fighting battles? Read on and find out.

Pages and Squires

Most knights were the sons of noblemen. They began training to become knights when they were even younger than you are now. By the time a lord's son was seven or eight years old, he would be sent away from the castle or manor to live with a relative, such as an uncle, or with his father's overlord—the person who had granted his father a fief. Why was he sent away?

It was here, in his new home, that the young boy started his training as a knight. In the first stage of training, the young boy served as a pageboy. A pageboy had to wait on tables and learn the manners of a nobleman. Most important, the pageboy was required always to be courteous to those of higher rank. Pages practiced their riding skills and fighting with toy swords. A knight had to know how to fight when tired and in pain, so pages practiced until they were exhausted.

When a page was about 12, he would become a squire. A squire was a personal servant to a particular knight. He went everywhere with the knight, cleaned the knight's armor and weapons, and cared for his horse. One of his most important jobs was helping the knight into his armor!

Becoming a Knight

Depending on his rank, the squire might be knighted any time between the ages of 16 and 20. Often a young man of high rank was knighted at an earlier age. Normally, a young man was knighted in a solemn ceremony. He stayed up all night, praying that he would be a worthy knight. Then he would be presented with spurs, a sword, a shield, and a helmet. His sponsor, usually the lord who had taken him in as a page, would tap him lightly on the shoulder with a sword and dub him Sir Something-or-Other.

During wartime the ceremony might not be so elaborate. There would be no time to stay up all night and pray. A young man simply might be handed a helmet and a sword, be tapped on the shoulder by a higher-ranking man, and sent into battle.

Not all knights were born into noble families. The rank of knight was one of the only positions of nobility that a poor man could hope to attain. Since nobles were usually desperate for good fighting men, a soldier who showed bravery in battle would occasionally be made a knight as a reward.

Life of a Knight

An armored knight on horseback was a great fighting machine. Arrows from enemy archers could bounce harmlessly off the steel plates. The armor also protected him from an enemy knight's sword and lance, a long wooden, metal-tipped pole.

In the early Middle Ages, armor was made of sheets of chain mail—metal rings—reinforced with plates of steel in key areas. A shirt of chain weighed about 25 pounds. Under the mail, the knight wore a shell of thick, hard leather.

By 1400, chain mail was replaced by hinged and fitted steel plates that covered a knight from head to foot. A suit of armor could weigh as much as 65 pounds. It was not easy to move around in these metal suits. That's why knights needed help getting into the saddle by their squires. But learning to move quickly in armor was a skill that knights had to learn if they were going to survive. On horseback, a knight was a dangerous soldier. If a knight fell off his horse, however, he was a sitting duck, unable to stand up quickly without help. After a fierce battle, a knight would sometimes need the help of a black-smith to get his dented helmet off his head.

Tournaments and Chivalry

Knights had to stay in shape to face the challenges of battle. During peacetime, knights held **tournaments**.

A tournament was a festive time for every-one on the lord's manor. Colorful banners would blow in the breeze on the tournament grounds. Knights painted colorful and complex designs on shields and banners to identify themselves and their families. A tournament would often attract knights and guests from surrounding castles. Lords and ladies wore their finest robes as they watched their favorite knights charge toward each other on horseback. The goal of the competition was to use a lance to knock the opposing knight off his horse. This was called jousting. Nobles and serfs alike would bet money on their favorite knight to win the competition.

> **vocabulary**
> **tournament** a staged battle fought by knights for money and honor without the intention to wound or kill

Tournaments were staged battles where knights could show how skillful they were.

Men of Honor

In the early Middle Ages, some knights could be a problem for their lords. After all, they were armed, violent men who settled arguments with their swords. They were the lord's vassals, and their job was to protect the lord from his enemies. But often lords felt threatened by their own knights.

To control the knights and their dangerous behavior, lords created a set of rules that knights should follow. These rules were called the **Code of Chivalry**. Knights were supposed to be generous, courteous, loyal, and honorable.

The Code of Chivalry required knights to follow certain rules of fighting. If a knight surrendered, he couldn't try to escape. He had to fight fairly. He could not cheat.

Chivalry also required knights to be courteous to women. A part of the code called for knights to show courtly love to a lady. A knight would pledge his honor to a lady and would perform acts of bravery to win her approval. The knight called himself his lady's vassal, placing himself below her just as a vassal placed himself below a lord. A knight who fought in a tournament would often tie his lady's scarf to his helmet to show that he was fighting on her behalf.

People loved to hear romantic stories about the adventures of knights and their ladies. **Troubadours** wrote long songs that told the stories of courtly lovers, and minstrels traveled about, singing and performing these songs for those who would pay to listen.

A knight was also expected to pledge his honor and respect to a lady.

The End of the Mounted Knight

What happened to knights? Remember you read earlier that castles became useless as armies started using cannons. The same thing happened to knights. Steel armor was fine protection against arrows and swords. But it was useless against cannonballs and bullets. However, knights did not disappear completely. Rulers continued to offer knighthood to men who had provided services to their kingdoms other than fighting. Explorers, artists, and scientists could become knights for outstanding achievements in their fields. Indeed, in Great Britain famous people are still awarded knighthoods today.

> **vocabulary**
> **Code of Chivalry** a set of rules for knights
> **troubadour** a person who composed poems that were set to music

 **The Medieval Majority** Before the 1300s, most people in medieval Europe were not lords or knights (or their wives). The vast majority were serfs. As you learned, serfs were the common people who lived on the manor estates and worked the land for the lord.

In fact, serfs came with the land. If a manor changed hands, the serfs who lived on the land went with it. If you bought the turf, you got the serfs, too.

If you're thinking that being a serf sounds something like being a slave, you're on the right track. Serfs were a little like slaves. One important difference was that a serf had the right to keep what was left over after paying whatever he owed to his lord. Also, serfs could pass their land on to their children.

Slaves had been common in the Roman Empire. However, as more and more members of the barbarian tribes became Christian, the church began to complain about slavery. The church at this time was not absolutely opposed to slavery, but it was opposed to enslaving Christians. As a result, many people who had been slaves were freed. These men were known as freedmen.

Unfortunately, these freedmen were not in a position to make much use of their freedom. Since they had been slaves all their lives, they generally had no money. Even if they could have purchased land, they probably would not have been able to protect themselves against warring tribes and powerful lords. Therefore, many freedmen decided to trade freedom for security by placing themselves under the protection of a feudal lord. They became serfs.

Indeed, even free peasants who may have owned their own land often gave up their independence to become serfs. Like the former slaves, these small landowners were outside the feudal support system and had no way to protect themselves from bandits, invaders, and neighboring lords. So, many of them willingly became serfs of a powerful lord. But not all peasants gave up their freedom.

All serfs led a hard life. Lords were supposed to protect their serfs, but if a lord treated a serf unfairly, about all he could do was abandon his land and flee. Serfs had to work extremely hard, and they kept little of what they grew or made.

The Life of a Serf

Serfs "belonged" to the land, and they lived close to the land. They spent their days digging in the soil to grow things. They had no soap to wash themselves, so their hands and bodies were often covered with dirt. They often had only one set of clothes, so they didn't wash their clothes, either. They wore the same clothes, no matter how caked with dirt and mud they became, until the clothes fell apart.

The house of a serf was typically made of earth. By around the year 1000, wood was hard to come by in parts of Europe. So serf houses were made of a frame of wood, with a mixture of mud and straw spread in between the wooden beams. The roof of the house was made of straw, and the floor was dirt. In wet weather, the floor was mud.

Serfs slept on the floor, perhaps with a layer of straw to provide a little bit of cushioning and warmth. They lived with their animals—chickens, sheep, and pigs. There was no fireplace—just a hearth in the middle of the floor, with smoke drifting up through a hole in the roof. The huts were smelly and smoky.

The life of a serf wasn't all work; there was time for fun and games.

Serfs spent many of their days working for the lord of the manor: plowing his fields, planting his seeds, harvesting his crops, and stomping his grapes to make wine. Women were often in charge of smaller livestock. They would shear the master's sheep, spin the wool into yarn, and weave it into cloth. Women also had the job of tending the family vegetable garden and caring for the children.

While the serfs prepared food and goods for the master, their own lives were very poor. They lived mostly on bread, vegetables, and ale or beer. As time passed, medieval serfs probably ate less meat, although women's diets improved after about the year 1000. This helped them live longer and bear more children, causing Europe's population to grow rapidly.

If serfs got sick, they depended on village healers, who used local herbs for healing. (Lords might have a professional physician, though his cures probably didn't work much better.) But serfs who didn't feel well didn't get much time to rest—they could be fined or whipped if they didn't work hard.

All peasants—serf or free—faced many difficulties. But there were still some good times in their hard lives.

Holidays

Just as we enjoy holidays today, people also enjoyed them in the Middle Ages. In fact, the word *holiday* comes from the "holy days" that were part of the calendar in the Middle Ages. Remember, the Church was a part of everyday life on the manor. People celebrated many more holidays than we do today. With Sundays, saints' days, and other holy days, there were about 100 days when everyone did little work.

On the holy days, the whole manor attended church. But there was usually more to these holy days than worship. The knightly tournaments you read about earlier were often held on holidays. People held parties, danced, and participated in sports such as bowling and wrestling. They watched jugglers and magicians and listened to traveling troubadours and minstrels. These sports and hobbies gave villagers something to look forward to and lightened the load of serfdom.

ASerf Goes to the City Now that you've read about the difficulties of a serf's life, you will not be surprised to hear that many serfs ran away from the manors to live in the cities. Imagine a serf who has lived his early life on a manor in the French countryside.

He spends his days in the field, working side by side with other serfs. Then one day this serf—let's call him Peter—is sent to the city to sell some firewood from the manor and bring the money back. He leaves the manor with a cart filled with firewood.

Before the trip Peter has heard many stories about life in the city, but he has never really believed them. Anyway, no stories can prepare him for the reality of the city.

For a young man who spends his days in open fields, the crowds of people pressing against him on all sides are a terrible shock. Peter would never have guessed that the whole world contained this many people. Walking with his horse and cart through the streets,

Peter feels as if he is being pushed and shoved all the way across the city.

Peter is astonished by the gangs of children at play, the women carrying baskets of fruit, and the men pushing small herds of sheep before them. And yet none of these people pay any attention to Peter whatsoever!

The city is filled with many churches. From all the churches you might think that the people who live here are very holy. That's what Peter thinks at first. But then he realizes they aren't. Instead, everywhere he looks, he sees thieves and beggars.

Peter watches as a group of actors present versions of Bible stories for people on the street. Is this a religious

The hustle and bustle around shops and shoppers added to the excitement of city life.

experience? No, Peter sees, as they pass the hat for people to put in money after each performance.

Even though it is a sunny day, Peter can't tell what time it is because the streets are shadowed by the rows of buildings. He listens for the toll of church bells to know the time.

Peter is excited by all the new sights, but he is also horrified by some of the new smells. As a serf, he is used to a certain amount of odors; but the city smells worse than anything he has encountered. People dump wastes from animals and people into open drains and ditches. Rainy weather has turned the dirt streets to stinky, messy marshes and mud. People selling meat and fish throw their unsold, rotting foods into the streets. Dogs and pigs roam around, trying to make a meal of such garbage. The river is filled with all kinds of garbage too, including dead animals. Nevertheless, Peter is fascinated with the city and city life.

After selling his firewood, Peter begins to make his way home to the manor. Peter cannot stop thinking about the alluring sights and sounds of the city. Then, he makes a decision. He will run away to live there. As he continues home, he begins to make plans. After a few weeks back on the manor, Peter escapes for the city and freedom.

What is Peter going to do in there? He is a farmer. How can he make his living in the city? Peter isn't sure, but he knows that much of the excitement in the streets is due to people selling and buying wares and services. The streets are crowded with shops of tailors, barbers, furriers, grocers, carpenters, cobblers, leather tanners, and bakers. These shops are more like market stalls opening right onto the street. In the back of the shops people make items to sell in the shops.

Peter wants to find a way to work in a shop. He goes from shop to shop, talking with shopkeepers and clerks about how the system works.

Guilds

In his discussions with shopkeepers and clerks, Peter discovers that each type of business is organized into a guild. For example, there are guilds for shoemakers, carpenters, hat makers, tailors, clockmakers, and jewelers. Master craftspersons, members of a guild, work together to make rules for operating their craft in the city. The guilds set standards for products and services that protect customers and workers alike.

Guilds require would-be members to train for a certain number of years with a guild member. Most start out as apprentices when they are children, helping the master at work.

When an apprentice learns some of the skills, he is promoted to **journeyman** and is allowed to make parts of the product. Finally, a journeyman will produce a "masterpiece," which is his finished product. For example, a shoemaker's masterpiece is a pair of finished shoes. The masterpiece is proof that a journeyman is competent to become a guild master himself.

Peter is too old to start as an apprentice, but he might look for work in the growing trade between cities. Merchants need people to carry their goods to other towns to sell. Trade has increased since the year 1000, as Europe has become somewhat safer from bandits and outlaws. For several centuries before, there was not very much travel or trade between areas in Europe.

The Growth of Trade and Cities

Many people preferred life in a town to life on a manor estate. Cities in Europe grew along with trade and business. London, Paris, Venice, and many other towns began to expand into larger cities. Still, even the largest (Paris) had fewer than 50,000 people.

The growth of towns and cities had an impact on local government as well as business. Unlike people on a manor, people in a town did not have a lord. French or English townspeople owed loyalty directly to the king. To establish a government, towns offered their king a sum of money for a **charter**. Charters granted townspeople permission to elect their own mayors, sheriffs, and other officials. However, the only people who could vote in these elections were the powerful merchants.

After 1000 the feudal lords began to lose power to the kings. Kings used the wealth from these towns and cities to become more powerful. And out of this change came some nations we know today—England, France, and Spain. The whole process took centuries. But the decline of feudalism and the erosion of the power of feudal lords began with the growth of middle-class power in the towns and cities.

> **vocabulary**
> **journeyman** an apprentice who is considered qualified to work in a particular trade
> **charter** a document given by a government or ruler to a group of people or a company

Churches, government buildings, guild halls, shops, and houses crowded behind the safety of city walls during the later Middle Ages.

How Women Lived Most of the people we've been talking about so far in the Middle Ages were men. There is not as much information about the lives of women in Europe during this time. However, a few women became very famous.

Most of the women of this time, like most of the men, were peasants and serfs. They had the same hard lives as their fathers, husbands, and brothers. Like boys, girls began doing farm work when they were about seven. They had to haul water, take care of younger children, and care for animals.

Adult women spent their days weaving, cooking, tending small animals, and caring for children. During busy times, women and men worked together in the fields, trying to grow enough food to pay their lords and keep their own families fed.

Poor Health

People in the Middle Ages did not know as much about medicine as we do today. Many died from diseases, and few lived as long as the average American today. Nobles and wealthy townspeople tended to be healthier than serfs just because they got enough to eat. But everyone suffered from lack of knowledge about germs, poor sanitation, and bad medical practices.

Women were at a special risk because of childbirth. Today, having a baby is a routine medical procedure. But in the Middle Ages it was very dangerous. Many mothers and their babies died in childbirth. To make matters worse, many of the children who survived the delivery did not make it to adulthood. So, there was much sadness and tragedy in life for women in the Middle Ages.

The Four Virtues—Fortitude, Prudence, Justice, and Temperance—are shown here teaching nuns how to take care of the sick.

Convent Leaders

Convents were like monasteries; the members, who were women, devoted their lives to God. And just as monasteries had a big impact on life in the Middle Ages, so did convents. Women in convents devoted their lives to prayer and to helping people. In the religious world of the Middle Ages, sending a daughter to a convent was thought of as an act of religious devotion.

The leader of a convent was called an abbess. Some leaders of convents became famous for their writings and even for their success at negotiating peace agreements among warring nobles. Matilda, the daughter of Holy Roman Emperor Otto I and the abbess of a convent, brought peace to much of Europe during her lifetime.

Hildegard of Bingen

One nun became famous in her time and her fame has lasted to our time. Her music is recorded frequently on CDs and can be found in most record stores and on the Internet. She is the earliest composer in history whose life story is known to us. In 1998, people in Vermont, California, Massachusetts, and Germany had parties to celebrate her 900th birthday. That's right—900th! Why was this woman so remarkable?

Hildegard of Bingen was born in 1098. She was a religious person from her earliest days. She began having religious visions when she was only three. When she was eight years old, her parents sent their religious daughter to live with a famous holy woman who was to be her teacher. In just a few years, though, people began hearing about Hildegard and her remarkable visions. Soon, a small group of young women came to live with Hildegard and Jutta, her teacher. This group started a convent.

Some of Hildegard's visions such as this of the tree of life were described and illustrated in books during her lifetime.

Throughout her life, Hildegard had remarkable visions. Today, some people think that her visions may have been caused by migraine headaches. But what made Hildegard special was not what caused her visions but what she did with those visions.

She had a vision when she was 42 in which "the heavens were opened and a blinding light of exceptional brilliance flowed through [her] entire brain. And so it kindled [her] whole heart and breast like a flame, not burning but warming . . . and suddenly [she] understood the meaning of expositions [explanations] of the books [holy books]. . . ."

Visions like this one and many others inspired Hildegard to write beautiful music that is still performed and recorded today.

She wrote poems and books based on her mystical visions. She wrote two medical books that were used for hundreds of years after her death.

Eventually, Hildegard started a new convent in the German town of Bingen. Her works were admired by the pope and by many other religious and political leaders. Arguing that women and men were equal in the eyes of God, she wrote, "God receives in baptism both sexes at all ages."

Trade and Learning

Many women went into business with their husbands, and others either began businesses by themselves or continued working alone after their husbands died. Historians have found records of women who worked as brewers, glassmakers, weavers, **coopers**, and **smiths**. Some women carried on these trades after the deaths of their husbands.

One important change during the Middle Ages that did not affect women was the development of universities. Universities sprang up in several big cities. The first ones were started in Paris and Bologna (Italy) in the 1200s, but other cities such as Padua, Prague, and Oxford soon followed their example. These universities advanced learning in many fields, but women were not allowed to go to them. This made it almost

vocabulary
cooper a person who makes barrels
smith a person who works with metals, such as a goldsmith, silversmith, tinsmith, or blacksmith

These women are selling the shoes and boots they made.

impossible for women to work in fields like law and medicine.

Women in convents, though, continued to share knowledge. Certain convents trained women to teach young children, and others trained women to provide health care and help to families.

Despite restrictions, a few women managed to leave a mark on the world. Margaret of Denmark and Matilda of Tuscany were two women rulers whose political skills brought them land and power. Rosvitha von Gandersheim (rahs VEE tah vahn GAHN durs hym) was a nun in Germany in the 900s. She wrote comic plays based on classical Greek and Roman dramas. Marie de France was a writer in France in the 1100s. We know very little about her except for the long poems she wrote about knights and courtly love.

Christine de Pisan

Christine de Pisan (krihs TEEN de pye SAHN), born in Venice in the 1300s, also wrote. Christine's family moved to Paris while she was still a baby. Her father was a famous scholar and was invited to work for the king of France. This was a great honor, for the court of the king of France was a very learned place. The move to Paris provided Christine with an opportunity. Unlike most women of her time, she was given the chance to get a very good education—and she took it. It's a good thing she did.

At first her life seemed to be going the way the lives of most young women went. She got married and had children. But then her husband and father died quickly, one after the other. Suddenly, Christine had three young children, a mother, and two younger brothers who depended on her. The king didn't offer to help Christine and her family with money, but she was allowed to keep using the king's library. That was a big help, because without a husband or father, Christine had to do the only thing she knew how to do. She began to write.

She started out with poems. Then she wrote about religion and history. She was especially interested in writing about women of the Middle Ages. Her most famous book was a history of women called *The Book of the City of Ladies.* Christine de Pisan also wrote a military manual. Her view was that armies should be used only for defense. It was a strange opinion in those warring times, but the book was read by many people.

She wrote books arguing that universities should accept women as students. "There is no doubt," she said, "that Nature provided [women] with the same qualities of body and mind found in the wisest and most learned men." If women did not receive an education, however, they could not develop those qualities.

Pisan's books were very popular. Her writings were translated into many languages. She hired women artists to illustrate her books, and she became the first European woman to earn her living as a writer.

After 29 years of writing, all the people Pisan needed to support were either grown up or dead. She retired to live in a convent. However, she wrote one book before she died—a long poem about Joan of Arc, a French woman who lived at the same time. Later you'll find out why this famous author broke her retirement to write about this remarkable young woman.

Christine de Pisan is kneeling to present one of her books to the queen of France.

William of Normandy In the 1000s, in a part of France called Normandy, there lived an eight-year-old boy named William. One day, William was a happy child, the son of a powerful lord, the duke of Normandy. The next day, William's father was dead.

Young William was named duke. Now, you might think that being a duke would be fun, but not for William. What it meant for him was that other powerful lords in Europe, men who had been friends of his father, wanted to kill him.

What was going on? Why would his father's friends want William dead? In the world of politics in the Middle Ages, the death of a great lord often was the cause of violence. As his father's oldest son, William was the rightful duke. But that didn't stop others from trying to kill him to become the duke themselves. William survived, thanks to help from the king of France.

Why is this story important? Because William, duke of Normandy, fought and won one of the most important battles in the Middle Ages, the Battle of Hastings. This battle changed the history of a nation and helped create the English language you are reading right now.

The Battle of Hastings

If you locate Normandy and the English Channel on a map, you can see that the English Channel is the body of water that flows between England and Europe. Normandy lies along the English Channel, just across from England. Today, Normandy is a section of France, but in the 1000s it was a duchy, a territory ruled by a duke. The king

of France, who was the duke's feudal lord, had little real power there.

In 1066 the king of England died. Several people claimed that they should be the next king of England. One was an English lord named Harold, who had himself crowned king. Another person with a claim to the throne was William, duke of Normandy.

In late September 1066, William and his army of knights and foot soldiers crossed the English Channel. King Harold was in the north of England, having just defeated another king who wanted to rule England. He and his army marched south and met William and the Norman forces on October 14, 1066, near the coastal town of Hastings. The English soldiers were in a line on a hillside. They turned back the first Norman charge. But when the Normans retreated, the English soldiers broke ranks and chased them. This was just the break William needed. He turned on the disorganized English army and

soundly defeated them. King Harold was killed in the battle.

William marched his army to London, the capital, and was crowned king. Now William, duke of Normandy, also became King William I of England. He is better known to history as William the Conqueror.

A New Language

William's conquest of England has had a big impact on our lives, even if we may never have lived in or even visited England. Before William arrived, most people in England spoke Anglo-Saxon (Old English). This was the language of the Germanic tribes who had arrived in England after the fall of the Roman Empire.

The Normans spoke an early form of French. At first, the common people of England spoke Anglo-Saxon and all the nobles (most of whom were the relatives and friends of William the Conqueror) spoke French. Eventually, the French and Anglo-Saxon languages blended. That is why English includes a mixture of French and Germanic words. Sometimes we even have two words for the same thing, one from the French and one from the Germanic languages. So it is with *cow* and *beef*. When we talk about cows, we are using a Germanic word that the Anglo-Saxon people used before William came to

England. When we sit down to eat beef, we are using a French word that was brought to England after the invasion of William and his knights.

Historical Documents

The Middle Ages were a long, long time ago. There are many people and events that we know very little about because there are few surviving records. But we know a good deal about England in the time of William the Conqueror because several important historical records have survived. Two of the most significant of these historical records are the Bayeux (bye YOO) Tapestry, part of which is pictured below, and the Domesday Book.

Sometimes, when a new ruler takes over, he leaves things pretty much as they were before. Not William! He started to change England from top to bottom. William threw many of the Anglo-Saxon lords off their lands and estates and replaced them with Norman friends who had fought with him at Hastings.

William wanted to know more about his new country. He ordered that a list be made of all the people and valuable items in the kingdom. The king's agents went all over England, visiting even the smallest villages and most distant settlements. They recorded

It is believed that one of William's brothers ordered the creation of the Bayeaux Tapestry as a record of the Battle of Hastings in pictures and words. Because of the tapestry, we can picture in our minds a battle that happened almost a thousand years ago.

the name of the lord of each territory, as well as the number of small landowners, knights, and serfs serving each feudal lord. They counted pigs, sheep, and other livestock and made notes about the forests in each region. If there was a mill or some other business in town, William's census takers made a note of it. They even kept a record of how many beehives there were in each territory.

The Domesday Book

This survey of William's kingdom was called the Domesday Book. It took several years and a lot of money to finish. But it was worth the expense, for the book let William know exactly who lived where. It allowed him to keep track of all the rent and taxes that were due to him.

But the Domesday Book was about more than taxes and money. William made sure that every lord listed in the book swore an oath of loyalty to him as the king of England. Anybody who did not cooperate with William's agents or refused to swear loyalty to the king was severely punished. The Domesday Book is a treasure for historians of the Middle Ages. It gives an accurate picture of a feudal kingdom over 900 years ago. For example, we know that there were two million people living in England during the reign of William I.

This is the Tower of London today.

One final item: What about the name, *Domesday?* It is actually an old-fashioned spelling of the word *Doomsday.* Some people think it was called that because people who did not cooperate with the king's agents were killed. But that is not the real reason. In fact, it was probably called the Domesday Book because doomsday was the biblical day of judgment and accounting. That was exactly what William's agents did when they arrived in a town—they counted up the people and judged how much everyone and everything was worth.

The Tower of London

William was also responsible for one of the most famous buildings in London, the Tower of London. A few months after winning the Battle of Hastings, William had a castle of earth and wood built on the north side of the Thames (temz) River in London. William's son added to this castle, and by 1100 it included a stone tower. Later kings continued to enlarge and fortify the castle. Over the years the Tower of London has been used as a fortress, a prison, a royal residence, and a place for storing treasure. Today, tourists visit it. It is one of the most famous symbols of the nation William helped build.

Weak Kings and Trouble in the Land William died in the year 1087. Several kings followed, all of them ruling England and parts of France. None of these kings were as strong as William the Conqueror, though, and that caused trouble in England.

Other nobles, seeing that William's successors were weak, tried to seize power. This led to constant warfare and a general breakdown of law and order. Without a strong king to hold them in line, the great lords just below the king made war on the king and each other in an effort to grow more powerful.

For serfs and people in towns and cities, these were hard times. Invading armies robbed people and killed anyone who resisted. Lords needed money to fight their wars, so they increased taxes on everyone. It was bad for business because trade could not be conducted safely. Towns and villages had to pay protection money to avoid being attacked. Then, they would be attacked by that lord's enemies anyway.

Henry II is shown here with all his royal symbols—holding the scepter and orb and wearing the crown.

A Strong King Makes Order

Once again, as in 1066, a hero arrived from across the English Channel. Henry II was the great-grandson of William the

Conqueror. But since he was only two when his grandfather Henry I died, the throne had been taken by one of his cousins. Even as a boy, Henry was involved in struggles over the throne of England. At first, his mother fought on his behalf. Finally, when he was 21, he won the support of some dissatisfied nobles. Henry was crowned King Henry II in Westminster Abbey, the greatest church in London, in December of 1154.

Bright and well educated, Henry spoke French and Latin, but he did not speak much English. Usually he was good-natured and gentle, but he had a terrible temper. It is said that once, when he was enraged with jealousy because someone had flattered one of his rivals, he ripped the covers from his bed and began to chew on his straw mattress!

A Man of Pleasure

Henry loved to hunt, and he loved to go hawking. Hawking was a sport that used trained falcons and birds of prey to capture other birds. These hunting birds were treated with care, like expensive hunting dogs. Henry loved to travel around with a favorite bird perched on a leather glove. He and his nobles often brought their trained birds to the banquet hall and fed them treats and morsels.

The King Is Number One

Henry was full of energy and ideas. As king, Henry had one goal. He was determined to end the wars that had plagued England in recent years and to make the king the strongest lord in England. Henry may have been an informal man of pleasure, but as king he dedicated his life to crushing his rivals and making sure the king would always be stronger than the lords. Henry did not waste time. One of his first acts as king was to take to the field of battle and go after lords who had grown too powerful.

Law and Order

Henry soon realized that he needed more than a good army to be a strong leader. He needed laws and government to make sure

It took patience to train a hawk, which is being allowed to fly free, to return with its prey.

the kingdom ran in an orderly manner. Henry turned his attention to the way the laws and courts worked in England.

The court system was very confusing. Lords were in charge of courts for certain types of crimes in certain places. The king was in charge of other courts, and the church was in charge of still other courts.

There were also different types of trials. In these trials people accused of crimes might be forced to "prove" their innocence through combat; or they might be forced to pick up a red-hot piece of iron in their bare hand. If the hand didn't heal quickly, he was guilty.

What a mess! Henry II set up a group of administrators who could run the legal system. Henry wanted to organize the system so criminals could not escape trials and punishment. He held several conferences with nobles and church leaders. In these meetings, Henry ordered a fairer legal system and the right to trial by **jury**. The job of people on a jury is to hear evidence in a trial and then to vote in secret whether they think the person accused of a crime is guilty or innocent. The jury system Henry began is still in use in England and the United States 900 years later.

Other Improvements

Henry made many other changes in his effort to make the king more powerful. Remember how vassals owed their lord military service? It was a centuries-old tradition of feudalism. But Henry realized it was not working. Lords who were not fully behind the king would take their time responding to the king's call for soldiers. Then, they would not send as many soldiers as they were supposed to.

Henry decided to change the law and started the *shield tax*. This meant that the lords had to send money instead of soldiers. Henry could then use the money to hire his own soldiers, who would be ready to fight and loyal to the king.

Henry also started a program of rebuilding castles. Henry built stone castles and made sure everyone understood that these were the king's castles. And the king could decide who lived there.

A Long Line of Kings

Henry and the kings who came after him were known as the Plantagenet (plan TAJ uh-niht) dynasty, or rulers belonging to the same family. The name *Plantagenet* probably came from a yellow flower called *Planta genista* that Henry's father liked to wear as a sort of badge or emblem. Henry II was the first Plantagenet king of England and is considered

> **vocabulary**
> **jury** a group of people who hear evidence in a trial and then vote on the guilt or innocence of the accused

Setting up a uniform system of laws and courts was probably Henry II's greatest accomplishment.

to have been the greatest of his line. All of them were known for their intelligence, energy, creative drive, quick anger, and strong sense of justice.

Henry's strong will and quick temper helped him accomplish all that he did as king. But these traits also caused problems. In the next lesson you will learn how Henry's hot temper led him into conflict with the most powerful priest in England.

15 Thomas Becket

A **Hard-Working Man** Henry II depended on a group of trusted advisors to help him run his large kingdom. The one he relied on most was named Thomas Becket. (You sometimes will see his name written Thomas à Becket.)

Becket was not born in a noble household. He was the son of a merchant. Becket became a priest, and through hard work and intelligence he began to rise through the ranks of the Church. At the same time, he also began to work his way up in the world of politics.

In 1154, one of the first acts of the newly crowned King Henry II was to appoint Thomas Becket to the job of chancellor. The chancellor was the king's highest advisor.

This was an important job. Becket worked hard, but he also enjoyed his hard-earned position. His household soon became as grand as any in the kingdom. In fact, Becket's house in London became known as the place to be. King Henry didn't care much for hosting fancy feasts. But everyone, including the king and queen, went to Becket's for a good time. He had a grand banquet hall with a high ceiling. In those days, people thought that eating raw fruit was unhealthy and that vegetables were for the poor. So, for the rich, meals consisted of meat, poultry, and breads.

But what meats and poultries! These nobles didn't live on chicken and roast beef. The platters in Becket's household carried starlings, seagulls, herons, and storks. Peacocks were roasted and presented with their spectacular tail feathers inserted in the roast. A roasted swan was arranged on a bed of green-tinted pastry so that it looked as if the bird were gliding over a pond.

Thomas Becket knew how to throw a good party. Most of his friends thought of him as a man who loved fun and a good time. But in his personal life, he remained a serious, devout priest. He also worked hard at his job to help King Henry bring order to the kingdom.

Archbishop of Canterbury

Working closely together, Becket and Henry became good friends. Becket was 15 years older than Henry, but they got along well, and Becket gave the younger king lots of advice that helped him run his kingdom well. You already know that Henry was trying to solve some problems in the legal system of England. He wanted to get rid of some of the loopholes created by the separate court systems of the Church. When the man who was the archbishop of Canterbury died, Henry thought it would be a good idea to tell the pope that his good friend Thomas Becket should be appointed the archbishop of Canterbury.

Being the archbishop of Canterbury was a great honor and a big promotion. There was only one problem: Becket didn't want the job. It may have been a great honor, but Becket saw the trouble that would lie ahead.

Since the king and the Church were often in conflict, he knew that Church officials would see him as on the king's side instead of theirs. He also knew that if he were going to do his job well, he would have to take positions that opposed the king.

But when a king asks you to do something, it's hard to say no. Becket became archbishop of Canterbury. At first, he and King Henry got along despite some minor conflicts about the Church courts. To everyone's surprise, Becket took his new job very seriously. Most people did not know about the serious side of Thomas Becket. Now they saw who he really was. The big parties and banquets came to an end. Becket put aside his fancy robes and furs and wore simple clothes and coarsely woven shirts. He spent a lot of time praying, meditating, and studying the Bible.

Trouble and Tragedy

King Henry was surprised by the change in his friend's behavior. But he grew truly alarmed when Becket opposed the king on questions about the role of the Church in the legal system.

King Henry proposed a new law that took a great deal of power away from the Church's courts and gave it to the king. Henry let Becket know that he expected him to support the new law. Instead, the archbishop opposed the king.

Hot-tempered King Henry was enraged at the actions of his former friend. This was the beginning of a feud that, thanks to Henry's bad temper, just kept getting worse. Henry charged Becket with violating the law. He took some of Becket's castles and lands away. Becket felt so threatened he left England secretly and spent a few years living outside the country. Twice they tried to end their conflict, but again and again they quarreled. Eventually, the pope ordered the king to end his quarrel with the archbishop or face **excommunication**. Henry gave in because he could not risk the anger of the pope.

Becket Returns

Becket felt it was safe to come back to England. King Henry was known for his bad temper, and Becket for his stubbornness. This was a recipe for trouble. And the trouble came soon enough. Shortly after he returned to England, Becket excommunicated some powerful nobles who were friends of the king.

> **vocabulary**
> **excommunication**
> the punishment of not allowing someone to continue as a member of the Church

This caused Henry to explode again. One night in December of 1170, Henry was at a castle in Normandy. In a fit of anger, he cried out, "Will no one rid me of this upstart priest?" No one really knows what Henry meant by these words. Were his words a casual expression of anger, or did Henry really want to be rid of Becket?

It so happened that four young knights, hotheaded and eager for the king's favor, heard the king speak. And they took his words as a serious call for action.

Slipping out of the castle that night, the knights found a boat to take them across the English Channel. At the cathedral in Canterbury, they found Becket conducting a religious service. The heavily armed knights expected Becket to be afraid and beg for his life. Becket did not run. He only began to struggle when the four rowdy men tried to drag him out of the cathedral. He declared himself "ready to die for my Lord," and then the knights hacked him to death, right there in the cathedral.

Thomas Becket was murdered on the altar of Canterbury Cathedral.

Reaction

The murder shocked all of Europe, but few were more upset by the crime than Henry himself. Just as Becket himself had done on becoming archbishop, Henry removed his fine clothing and dressed in sackcloth, a rough, uncomfortable cloth made of the hair of animals and other coarse fibers. He poured ashes over his head. Like dressing in sackcloth, this was a way to show sorrow. He refused to eat or sleep. He exiled himself for six months and then asked to be whipped.

Finally, he made a **pilgrimage** to Canterbury. When he was three miles from the cathedral, he got off his horse and removed his shoes. The king walked the last three miles barefoot. By the time he arrived, "his footsteps . . . seemed to be covered in blood . . . for his tender feet being cut by the hard stones, a great quantity of blood flowed from them on to the ground."

> **vocabulary**
> **pilgrimage** a journey undertaken for a religious purpose

Three years after his murder, Becket was made a saint by the Church. His tomb in Canterbury Cathedral became the most popular shrine in England. Henry was rid of his "upstart priest," but he had also lost one of his best friends. Yet Henry would find even more trouble before his rule had ended. This time, the source would be someone who was even closer to him than his old friend Becket.

People who visited and prayed at Becket's shrine often wore a badge like this one to show that they had been there.

The Queen of France Eleanor of Aquitaine was a woman who had everything. She was beautiful, charming, intelligent, and came from a powerful family. She could read and write (unusual for a girl in the 1100s), play the harp, and ride a horse as well as a boy.

But the most important thing that Eleanor had was land. She was the duchess of Aquitaine (AK wih tayn), one of the largest and richest regions of what is now France. Aquitaine was a region rich in rivers (its name came from the Roman word for "land of waters"), olive groves, vineyards, wheat fields, orchards, and forests.

As duchess, she was a vassal of the king of France; but she controlled more land than he did.

Still, she had to do what the king said. So when the king told the 15-year-old Eleanor that she was going to marry Louis, his 16-year-old son, whom she had never met, she didn't even question it. Eleanor had always known that she would marry a young nobleman some day and that her marriage would be based on land rather than love. Shortly after her marriage, the old king died and Louis became king of France. Eleanor became the queen.

At first, the two teenagers got along quite well, but disappointments followed. Eleanor produced two girls instead of the son the king needed to follow him on the throne. She hated the royal castle in Paris, which struck her as a cold, dreary place compared with sunny Aquitaine. Louis was not as bold and dashing a knight as Eleanor's father and grandfather had been. To make things worse,

Louis got more and more interested in religion, and life in Paris became more and more dull for Eleanor. Was she looking around for a new husband? No one really knew, but one day a young nobleman named Henry came to Paris.

The End of a Royal Marriage

You've met Henry before. The young man Eleanor saw was the same handsome, energetic, and charming man who later became Henry II. When Eleanor met him, he wasn't yet king of England. He was Henry of Anjou (ahn ZHOO), and he controlled the lands north of Eleanor's Aquitaine. The king of France saw Henry as his chief rival for power. Little did he know how much of a rival Henry would be.

Shortly after she met Henry, Eleanor asked for an annulment, or a cancellation, of her marriage to Louis. King Louis was sad that she wanted to end the marriage; he still loved Eleanor. But Louis was unhappy about the marriage, too. Their failure to produce a son was a serious issue. The religious king wondered whether that failure was a sign of God's displeasure, as Eleanor claimed. After 15 years of marriage, the marriage was annulled, and Louis and Eleanor went their separate ways.

Eleanor returned to Aquitaine. Even if she had wanted to remain unmarried for a while, Eleanor soon saw that it was impossible. She was simply too valuable. More than one knight tried to kidnap her and force her to marry him. Eleanor needed the protection of a husband.

Queen of England

No one knows for sure when or how Henry and Eleanor agreed to marry or who made the first proposal. Yet, two months after the annulment of her marriage to Louis, Eleanor and Henry were married.

These two were far better suited to each other than Eleanor and Louis had been. Henry and Eleanor were both intelligent, bold, and spirited people who admired learning and literature and enjoyed power. In the first 13 years of her marriage to Henry, Eleanor had eight children with Henry, including five sons.

Together, they were the most powerful couple in Europe. The combination of their lands gave Henry the knights, ships, and power he needed to sail across the Channel and claim the throne of England.

For 14 years, Henry and Eleanor ruled together over their kingdom that stretched from Scotland to Spain. Look at the map to see what lands they controlled.

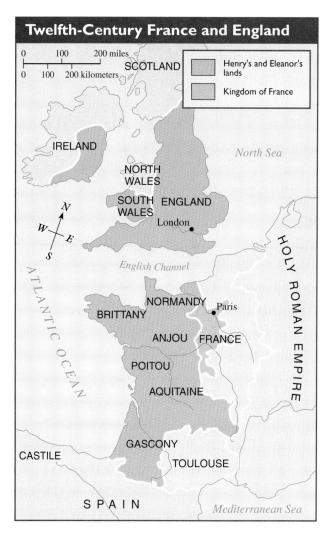

Twelfth-Century France and England

0   100   200 miles
0   100   200 kilometers

SCOTLAND

IRELAND

North Sea

NORTH WALES

SOUTH WALES   ENGLAND

London

English Channel

ATLANTIC OCEAN

NORMANDY   Paris

BRITTANY

ANJOU   FRANCE

POITOU

AQUITAINE

HOLY ROMAN EMPIRE

CASTLE

GASCONY

TOULOUSE

S P A I N   *Mediterranean Sea*

Henry's and Eleanor's lands

Kingdom of France

You can see how much land Henry and Eleanor controlled.

Eleanor was 11 years older than Henry, and at last their marriage began to fail. Eleanor returned to Aquitaine with her children. It wasn't long before some of her sons were teenagers. The young sons were impatient for power of their own. Henry gave them titles but no power. Eleanor encouraged her sons to think about the day when they could oppose their father.

Meanwhile, Eleanor held court in Aquitaine. She hired the best poets and troubadours to entertain her and her castle full of teenaged children and their friends. She favored stories of courtly love in which brave young knights performed feats of courage for their ladies. She encouraged her sons to be brave and dashing, but she also demanded courtesy and witty conversation in her court. It was the most civilized place in Europe.

Royal Rivals

The murder of Thomas Becket was a turning point in Henry II's rule of England. Many powerful nobles in England blamed Henry for Becket's murder. Eleanor saw an opportunity and encouraged her sons to take advantage of the king's new weakness and rebel against him. With their mother's help, the sons were able to get the help of several powerful nobles eager to strike back against the king. Remember, it was King Henry who had just recently stripped them of their power.

The sons, with the help of several nobles, did lead a rebellion against their father. But Henry was still a master warrior. Henry put down the rebellion and placed Eleanor under house arrest, making her a prisoner in one of his castles. There she stayed until his death some 15 years later.

King Richard I

At Henry's death, his and Eleanor's eldest son, Richard, became king. Richard immediately had his mother freed. The new king was very close to his mother. And Eleanor saw many of the same qualities in Richard that she had first admired in Henry. He was dashing, handsome, adventurous, and energetic. Richard would have been a great king, except for one important thing: He did not have his father's gift for governing. Henry may have been quick to anger, but he was a gifted ruler who knew how to solve problems.

During his ten years as king, Richard the Lionhearted, as he was called, hardly set foot in England. He was too busy leading crusades against the Muslims, having adventures, and fighting wars. At one point he was taken prisoner and held for ransom. Eleanor raised the money to get him out of prison.

If the king was away so much, who ruled England while he was gone? His mother, Queen Eleanor, that's who. As Henry II had done, she worked on solving problems in England. She introduced a system of uniform coins, weights, and measures. She also did away with some unfair rules. These reforms made her popular with her subjects.

When Richard was killed during one of his adventures, Eleanor was heartbroken. She was nearly 80 now and ready to take a rest at the end of a rich and long life. Eleanor retired to a convent, where she died at the age of 82.

The statue of Queen Eleanor on her tomb is holding a book, which shows just how unusual a woman of her time she was.

17 The Magna Carta

The Landless Son The youngest child of Eleanor of Aquitaine and Henry II was a boy named John. Although John would become Henry's favorite (perhaps because he was not as close to his mother as the other boys), Henry had already given his most valuable fiefs to his other sons.

As a young man, John was given the nickname "John Lackland," because he did not have any land of his own. No one expected John to become king because he had so many older brothers who would come to the throne before he did. In fact, when John was very young, he was sent to be raised in a monastery. Like Hildegard of Bingen, he was supposed to dedicate his life to God. All of that changed, however.

Except for Richard, all of John's older brothers died before reaching the throne. When Richard died, the 32-year-old John was the sole surviving son of Henry II, so he became king of England.

For many centuries, John was considered the worst king in English history by historians. Nowadays, many say that he wasn't such a terrible king, but he did make some mistakes. Like other Plantagenet kings, he was intelligent and hard-working, with a strong sense of justice. Nonetheless, people did not seem to trust him, and intelligence and hard work were not enough to win wars.

A Series of Defeats

Five years after John took the throne, the king of France attacked Normandy and Anjou. These were the lands that Henry II brought to his marriage with Eleanor. John was unable to defend the lands. One reason

was that his nobles did not like or trust him enough to fight for him.

It was bad enough that John lost important lands to the French king, but now he wanted his nobles to pay higher taxes to cover the costs of the war. He raised their taxes. If nobles refused to pay, or could not pay, he took hostages. In other words, he might hold a relative or important servant prisoner until the baron paid up. King John also demanded taxes from people who lived in cities, especially wealthy merchants. This put the merchants on the side of the nobles, or barons.

John seemed to have a special talent for making enemies. Now that he had the barons and powerful townspeople angry with him, he made enemies with the pope. King John refused to agree to the man the pope wanted to become archbishop of Canterbury. It was not a wise decision on John's part. The pope, Innocent III, was probably the most powerful man in Europe at this time. He fought back with all the weapons he had.

After John seized property that belonged to the Church, the pope ordered all the churches in England closed. Priests refused to perform any sacraments, or holy ceremonies. No weddings, funerals, or baptisms could be performed. People could not confess their sins and be forgiven. And it was all King John's fault! Then, Innocent excommunicated the king. John had no choice but to give in. This was a costly defeat. First, he agreed to recognize the pope's choice as archbishop. Then, John surrendered England to the pope and became his vassal. The pope returned England to John as his fief. It was humiliating.

A Great Charter

Peace with the Church did not satisfy the demands of the angry barons and townspeople. In 1215 they prepared a list of demands known as the Magna Carta, which is Latin for "great charter." It laid out rules for what the king could and could not do to nobles, citizens, and the Church. The barons said they would go to war against John if he did not sign the document. When he saw he could not defeat them, John agreed to meet the demands of the barons.

At a meeting in a meadow outside London, John signed the Magna Carta. Copies were made by hand and carried all over the kingdom. John died the next year of a fever as a new war raged through his kingdom. Over the next eleven years, the charter was revised several times. The final version was signed in 1225 by John's son, Henry III.

Why is the Magna Carta important? It is an important document in the history of the rule of law. In the Magna Carta a king agreed that he had to rule according to laws. Some

This is a nineteenth-century painting of a very important event in English history—the signing of the Magna Carta. One of ten existing copies of the Magna Carta is shown here.

of the Magna Carta's principles lasted through the centuries that followed.

A few ideas in our Constitution can be traced back directly to the Magna Carta. Modern democracy, with its emphasis on freedoms and rights, was still a long way in the future, but one of the first steps was taken when a group of barons got King John to sign the Magna Carta in a field outside the city of London.

London Bridge

King John is also remembered for the construction of the first stone bridge across the Thames River in London. The bridge was completed in 1209 and stood for 600 years. It was not just a way to get across the river; it included two rows of houses and 140 shops. More than 500 years would pass before another stone bridge was constructed across the Thames in London.

England's First Parliament King John died the year after he signed the Magna Carta. His son Henry III was only nine years old, so England was ruled by a council of barons until Henry was old enough to rule.

During these years of rule by the council, barons settled their disputes in discussions rather than by going to war. Instead of hard times, England enjoyed peace.

Henry's grandfather, Henry II, had created a system of government that worked well. For centuries, England had been divided into counties. Under Henry II's system of government, each county had a sheriff who managed local affairs. The whole country was divided into six **circuits**, or districts. Each circuit had three judges. All the judges enforced the same laws, which made the country seem more unified.

> **vocabulary**
> **circuit** an area or district through which a judge travels to hold court sessions

Once Henry III was old enough to rule, there were problems. He forgot things. He didn't get things done that he was supposed to do. He also gave many jobs in the government to his wife's friends and relatives. Once again the barons rebelled, as they had against Henry's father, King John. They demanded that the king allow a council of barons to rule. At first, Henry agreed. Then he changed his mind, and war broke out between the king and some of the barons.

England's First Parliament

After capturing King Henry III, Simon de Montfort, the leader of the barons' revolt, tried something new. He called a meeting of land-owning nobles, leaders of the Church, knights, and citizens from the towns to pass laws and run the country. Since it was not practical for everyone to come, Montfort had each group vote for representatives who would come to the meeting.

This historic meeting was the first time that representatives from all classes, except serfs, met together to make decisions. This was the beginning of England's parliament system. More than 100 people met for two months. Although it was not democratic by modern standards, it was a new idea. This first parliament was an exciting but short-lived affair. King Henry escaped from capture. His army defeated the rebels and killed Simon de Montfort. The parliament was disbanded.

The Model Parliament

The next king, Edward I, learned from the mistakes of his father, Henry III, and his grandfather John. Edward was fighting a war to keep Aquitaine from being taken away by the French. He was building expensive castles in Wales, and he was also trying to conquer Scotland. These projects cost a lot of money. Instead of ordering people to pay taxes the way King John had, Edward decided to try something different. Using the idea of Simon de Montfort's parliament, he called together representatives from throughout his kingdom. He hoped to win their cooperation in raising money for his projects.

In 1295, what became known as the Model Parliament met in Westminster, now part of London. It included two knights from each county and two citizens from each city and town. These representatives were elected, not appointed. Also attending were representatives sent by priests, as well as barons, nobles, and bishops. The Model Parliament included some prominent women as well as men. It has become known as the Model Parliament because every Parliament in England since then has been based on the model of this one.

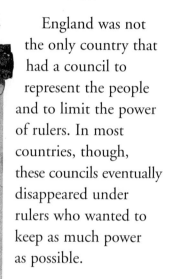

King Edward, surrounded by a king of Scotland, a prince of Wales, Church leaders, and representatives of nobles and townspeople, presides at the Model Parliament.

Edward was a wise king. He concluded that he would be more likely to get the money he needed and avoid bad feelings if he directed his requests to the representatives in Parliament. His plan worked. Parliament agreed to give the king the money he needed. But once Edward started asking for money from Parliament, things began to change.

People began to expect the king always to ask Parliament for money. Eventually, the idea sprang up that the king couldn't impose taxes without first getting the approval of Parliament. This was not the king's idea of what should be done. Friction developed between the king and Parliament.

Parliament's power continued to grow. In the 1300s, Parliament divided into two houses. The representatives from the towns and cities formed their own section that became known as the House of Commons. The barons and nobles became the House of Lords.

England was not the only country that had a council to represent the people and to limit the power of rulers. In most countries, though, these councils eventually disappeared under rulers who wanted to keep as much power as possible.

In England, Parliament has continued in much the same form through the centuries. Well into the 1600s the king and Parliament continued to struggle over power. Sometimes, Parliament held the upper hand. Other times, the king was stronger.

Parliament Today

Today, the House of Commons has 650 elected representatives. Both houses of Parliament meet in the Great Palace on the Thames River. This building was rebuilt in the mid-1900s, but it includes Westminster Hall, built in 1099. The houses of Parliament are among of the most famous landmarks in London.

An Unstable Situation Sometimes, being closely related can be a cause of confusion and even conflict. That certainly was the case in England and France during the Middle Ages. For many generations the rulers of England actually spoke French.

Henry II, for example, was one of the great kings of England. He spoke French much better than he spoke English.

As strange as it sounds, the king of England and many of the powerful English nobles were also vassals of the king of France. You see, many years earlier the ancestors of these English nobles had received large grants of land from the king of France, and this meant that they and their heirs owed loyalty to the king across the English Channel.

This became a very big problem when the kings of England and France went to war. Many nobles were vassals of both kings and owed loyalty to both.

Here was another complicated part of feudalism: All these nobles and monarchs could only marry other monarchs and high-ranking nobles. Therefore, the kings and dukes of almost every part of Europe were related to one another. This caused some serious confusion when a king died. In fact, most wars were fought over the succession, or the order in which people took the throne. Remember the Battle of Hastings?

In the 1300s the king of France died, leaving no sons to take his place on the throne. The mother of the king of England had been the sister of the king of France who had just died. That meant that the king of England,

Edward III, was the nephew of the recently deceased king of France. The English king claimed the throne of France, but nobody in France accepted his claim. In fact, the French throne had previously been claimed by Philip of Valois (vah LWAH), a nobleman. This conflict over the French throne was the event that started the Hundred Years' War.

A Misleading Name

The Hundred Years' War is a misleading name in at least two ways. First of all, the Hundred Years' War lasted more than a hundred years. It lasted 116 years to be exact. Second, the Hundred Years' War was not a single war. It was several smaller wars fought between England and France. War did not go on all the time during the 116 years from 1337 to 1453. There were **truces** that lasted up to 25 years.

When the Hundred Years' War began, France was by far the richest and most powerful kingdom in Europe. It was rich in farming and grazing land. French castles and churches were the marvel of Europe.

England, on the other hand, was a small island with a harsher climate, fewer people, and much less wealth than France. So it is no surprise that the king of

> **vocabulary**
> **truce** an agreement to stop fighting

France made a terrible mistake: He was overconfident. He misjudged England and overlooked some of the strengths of the island nation.

One of the things that England had going for it was the wool trade. The climate of England was bad for growing crops, but it was good for raising sheep. The wool from these sheep provided a good income. It also caused Flanders, a cloth-producing region of northern France, to side with England.

In military terms it looked like France had a big advantage. First, most of the war was fought in France, so the French were fighting on their home territory. Second, it was very expensive to ship armored knights and horses across the English Channel to France. Finally, in most battles, the French had a big advantage because they had many more knights.

But once again, the English were stronger than they appeared. England was the first nation to make use of a new kind of bow called the longbow. With the longbow, archers could shoot arrows a longer distance with greater power. In fact, arrows shot from a longbow could cut through armor.

To make a very long story short, the French misjudged their rivals. That is one of the reasons why a war that the French thought they could win quickly turned into a war that went on for such a long time.

Bloody Battlefields

The Hundred Years' War was a series of bloody, costly wars. Thousands of soldiers died on each side. The use of the longbow took away the great advantage that armored knights had previously enjoyed on the battlefield. English archers, when given the chance, used their weapons to mow down French knights.

One of the most famous battles of the war was fought at the French town of Agincourt (AJ ihn kor). A large, powerful French army cornered a small English army. The French were sure of victory. The English

The blue and red flag carried by the English soldiers on the right displays symbols of both England and France—the English lion and the French lily.

were sure they would be slaughtered by the French forces. But the superior tactics and powerful longbows of the English resulted in a horrible, bloody defeat for France.

The End of the War

The way armies fight at the end of a war is often very different from the way they fight at the beginning of the war. That certainly was the case in the Hundred Years' War. Remember how the longbow gave the English a military advantage?

Well, the French never stopped trying to come up with better weapons of their own. Around 1400 they did. The French developed cannons that were powerful, easy to move around, and accurate. Soon, French artillery gave them a big advantage.

When the fighting stopped, the French had won. England had to give up almost all the territory it had controlled in France.

Effects of the War

But the Hundred Years' War is more important for what happened to England and France than for the military results. Yes, France won the war and took back territory from England. But both countries were changed forever by the fighting.

The use of the cannon changed warfare in the Middle Ages.

France was left in terrible shape from the fighting. English soldiers, far from home, had routinely stolen and looted from French towns and farms. Soldiers also had held entire villages for ransom. They would capture a village, threaten to burn it and kill everyone in it if people in the surrounding villages didn't pay some money. All this looting and ransoming left France much poorer than it had been before the war. It also left a feeling of hatred between the French and the English that lasted for more than 400 years.

A Different World

The real winners of the war were the kings of both France and England. The deaths of so many knights weakened many noble families. The power of the noble barons was reduced, and kings in both countries became stronger.

The war also weakened the rule of feudalism. Towns and cities began to grow in size and power. They owed no loyalty to a feudal baron but to the king from whom they received their charter. So, instead of feeling loyal to their feudal lord, people felt loyal to their king and their country.

This feeling for their country led to another big change that affects us today. During the war the rulers of England and educated and wealthy people stopped speaking French and began speaking English. Books and documents began to be written in English.

History is always clearer when we look back from the present than it is to the people living through it. Although the people didn't know it at the time, a new world was being born.

**A Hero for the Ages** You have read about great kings and warriors. Now you are going to read about a great warrior who was certainly one of the greatest heroes of the entire Middle Ages. Her leadership turned the tide of battle in the Hundred Years' War. Her actions helped the French win a war they seemed certain to lose.

Yes, that's right, this great warrior was a woman, actually a teenager. She was a simple peasant girl, not a well-educated woman of noble birth. She was about the same size as most of you. But Joan of Arc became a giant in the history of the Middle Ages. Her story is still exciting to read more than 500 years after she lived.

Hope Returns

In the last lesson you read about how the English won battle after battle against the French in the Hundred Years' War. Yet, France seemed to have all the advantages in the war. But these advantages were of no use against the English. All the years of fighting and looting had left the French pretty hopeless and dispirited. It seemed as if they had lost the will to fight the English.

In battle after battle, 10 to 15 times as many French soldiers were killed as English soldiers. This was partly because the French had a very old-fashioned way of fighting. They treated war as a tournament, or game. They wanted to play fair, so they waited patiently on their horses until the English had set up their barricades of pointed stakes and had put all their archers into position. Then, when the English were ready, the French would attack. At that point the English would shower arrows on the advancing French horsemen. Shot from powerful longbows, the

sharp arrows could pierce the thin sheets of armor of the French knights, most of whom never even got close enough to use their swords on the English.

In the last decades of the war, though, the French regained their courage and their will to fight. They stopped fighting to be fair and started fighting to win. This change came from a most unexpected source: a simple girl named Jeanne. In English we call her Joan. Joan believed that God had given her the mission of driving the English out of France and restoring the French king to the throne.

Visions and Voices

Joan grew up in a small village called Domrémy (dohm REH mee). When she was about 13 years old, she began having visions of God and angels and hearing voices, which she believed to be the voices of God and the saints. At first, they simply told her to live a good life. As the years went by, however, she heard the voices more often. Finally, she understood that she was being told that God had chosen her to rescue the kingdom of France. Joan was 17.

Joan was stunned at this idea. She knew nothing about war or politics. Yet the voices continued. After the village of Domrémy was burned by the English, the voices became urgent and more specific. They told her that she should go to a nearby large town about

12 miles from her home. At this town, Joan was told to ask the help of the governor in reaching the man who was next in line to be king, the **dauphin** (doh FAN). The voices told Joan her mission was to free the city of Orléans (or-lay AHN), which was under siege by the English, and to see the dauphin crowned king of France.

The governor had no interest in meeting with her. So Joan simply stood outside his castle, praying and explaining to people why she had come.

Joan soon had a small group of supporters. One of them, a young soldier, gave her the clothes of a young man to put on. Someone else gave her a horse. Yet another person cut her hair for her. The governor finally agreed to see her. At first he laughed at her; but later, for reasons no one knows for sure, he changed his mind. He gave her a sword and permission to go to the dauphin. He gave her an archer, a royal messenger, and three servants. Her friend, the young soldier, and his squire came as well.

Joan is usually portrayed wearing the clothing and armor of a soldier.

A Victory at Orléans

Joan and her little band traveled through 350 miles of cold, flooded rivers and war-torn countryside. She was admitted into the grand hall of the castle where the dauphin was staying. It was filled with more than 300 knights and many courtiers dressed in fine clothes. The dauphin stood among them.

Legend has it that the dauphin was testing Joan by mingling with the crowd, but Joan surprised everyone by walking right up to him and kneeling before him. It may be that Joan had seen his picture before on coins or banners. Yet, it was impressive that a simple peasant girl could pick him out of such a crowd.

Joan was given a room in the castle, and she began to practice her fighting skills. A group of strong and even famous knights gathered around her. We can't explain how, but Joan soon had these famous warriors willing to do whatever she asked. All we can assume was that Joan's faith and her leadership inspired others to follow her. With an army of some 3,000 to 4,000 soldiers, Joan set off for Orléans.

The city had been under siege for nearly seven months. The English hadn't succeeded in capturing the city, but the French forces were weak and losing ground. As Joan rode through Orléans on the night of her arrival, townspeople carrying torches pressed around her. Rumors had spread through France that a young woman dressed as a boy had been sent by God to save them from the English.

Joan was eager to battle the English, but the French commander urged her to be patient as he assembled his troops. Joan agreed, but a few days later, just as she was settling down for an afternoon nap, she suddenly jumped up. "In God's name," she said, "my counsel [advisor] has told me I must attack the English." Her voices had spoken to her. She rode down to the gates of the city where she found French soldiers, wounded and bleeding, retreating from the English forces. When the French soldiers saw Joan on her horse, waving her white banner, a new spirit filled them. They turned around and headed back toward the English with such a surge of force that the English, who had been winning just a short time before, began to retreat.

The people of Orléans cheered the victorious Joan and her soldiers.

She predicted that she would be wounded, but she fought without a helmet so that her soldiers could see her. An arrow pierced her neck. She almost fainted with pain, but a few hours later she returned to the fight. After three days of fighting, the English were finally driven out of Orléans. The war was not over, but for the first time it seemed that the English might be defeated.

This was an important victory, but the sight of the blood and the corpses upset Joan. Though she thought that fighting was necessary to win the freedom of France, she demanded that her soldiers go to church, and she did not allow swearing or looting among her men.

A Crown for a King

Now Joan devoted herself to the next part of her mission. She returned to the dauphin and convinced him to travel to Reims (reemz). This was the city where French kings had been crowned for hundreds of years. The problem was that Reims was controlled by the Burgundians (bur GUN-dee unz) who were on the side of the English. When Joan arrived, however, the residents of the city had a change of heart. They cheered the dauphin. The Burgundian army quietly slipped out of town, and Charles, the dauphin, walked up the aisle of the great cathedral with Joan at his side. He would be dauphin no longer. He was crowned Charles VII, king of France. Joan was at the peak of her glory.

Politics and Prison

If the story of Joan of Arc were a fairy tale, she and King Charles VII would defeat the English and live happily ever after. In real life, politics entered the story.

Once he was crowned, the king began making deals behind Joan's back. Joan simply wanted to keep fighting until the English were driven out of France. But the king made deals with the Burgundians and the English without telling Joan.

In 1430, Joan was captured by Burgundian soldiers, who then sold her to the English. The English and Burgundians "were more joyous than if they had seized five hundred men-at-arms, for they feared no captain or leader as much as they had . . . feared [Joan]."

Trial and Death

Joan was thrown into prison and prepared for a trial. Because she claimed to hear the voice of God and the voices of saints, she was to be tried for heresy, the crime of going against the teachings of the Church. To prove this crime, they needed to find some people who were willing to repeat gossip or spread rumors, and they did. Finally, some churchmen who did not know Joan but who were either afraid of the bishop or hoped to gain from helping the English were summoned to try her. Day after day they questioned her. They focused most of their questions on the voices that Joan claimed to hear and on the fact that she wore men's clothing. For a woman to wear a man's clothing was a serious crime.

Joan conducted herself so well and answered so simply and truthfully that it was hard to make much of a case against her. But after weeks of questioning and accusations, the court sentenced her to death.

She was burned at the stake, a death she dreaded. "I would rather be beheaded seven times than burned," she said. As the fires licked at her, she gazed at a large cross that one of the spectators held before her. She called to Jesus, and then she was silent. Some people wept as she burned. An English person called out, "We have burned a saint."

Joan's death was a public event at which many people wept. She was nineteen years old.

Victory

Although Joan was dead, the tide of the war had turned. The French succeeded in driving the English out of all of their territories except the city of Calais.

Twenty years after her death, the Church held an investigation of her trial. After a complete review of the evidence, it was decided that the trial had been unfair. It was too late to help Joan, and no one involved in the unfair trial was ever punished, but Joan's reputation as a great hero was secure. For centuries, writers and artists have told her story in poems and plays and statues. In 1920 the Catholic Church declared the simple peasant girl a saint.

A Terrible Way to Die Imagine that you are a ten-year-old child living in Florence, Italy, in the year 1348. You're sent by your parents to a nearby market. As you wander about the busy marketplace, you overhear people talking. "It started in Sicily," one man says.

"No, no," says another man, "it started in the East. The Tartars began it."

The first man waves his hand impatiently. "No matter where it started. It's killed most of Sicily, and now it's coming here."

What on earth are these people talking about? You pull on the jacket sleeve of one of the men. "Sir, sir," you ask. "What are you talking about?"

The two men glance at one another. The man in the jacket turns to you and looks at you with stern eyes. "It's the Great Death, child. It's coming. Now, run home and tell your parents to get you and your brothers and sisters out of town."

Before much time had passed, you would learn a great deal more about the Great Death. All around you, people would die. Some would die very quickly, almost as though they were poisoned. Others would linger for three days or even six, most developing ugly growths the size of eggs in their armpits, neck, and lower body. Large red and black spots appeared on their skin. Some would fall into a coma. Others would seem to do a strange dance as their nervous system was attacked by the disease.

Nowhere to Run, Nowhere to Hide

The man who feared the worst would turn out to be right. The Great Death did come to Florence, and it killed more than half the people in the city.

The **plague** seems to have started in Asia in the 1320s. It was carried by ships to cities in Italy and France and to ports in Sicily in 1347. The next year it moved inland and attacked Italy, France, Spain, northern Africa, and Greece. There was still hope that it would stop, but eventually it covered northern Germany, Scotland, and the Scandinavian countries of Norway and Sweden. It reached all the way to Iceland and Greenland.

> **vocabulary**
> **plague** a highly contagious, usually fatal, disease that affects large numbers of people

Today, it is believed that the plague was spread by rats and fleas. Some scholars believe that the Black Death, as it is now called, was really a combination of three or four diseases spreading through Europe at roughly the same time.

Disappearing Villages

The worst outbreak of the Black Death only lasted four years. But when it was over, Europe was a very different place. It is estimated that about one third of the people in Europe, around 25 million people, died of the plague. It wasn't until 1600, about

250 years later, that Europe reached the population level that existed before the plague hit.

Some areas were hit harder than others. In some regions as many as two thirds of the population died. In England alone, about a thousand villages disappeared as a result of the plague. In some places there were not enough people remaining to bury the dead. People who survived moved to larger towns.

The Black Death was so severe that in many places there were not enough coffins and, often, no one to conduct church services.

Long-Term Effects

Once the Black Death had passed, people started to pick up the pieces. One positive result of so much death was the sudden labor shortage. Serfs could bargain for better working conditions. In fact, most serfs were able to buy their land and freedom. Within a hundred years, serfdom disappeared from Europe.

The shortage of workers also inspired people to try to invent labor-saving devices.

New types of water mills and windmills were invented, along with other new inventions like the printing press. Efforts to understand the horrors of the Black Death and to prevent it from happening again encouraged an interest in science and medicine.

The End of the Middle Ages

Remember how the Hundred Years' War helped weaken feudalism? The Black Death also helped weaken feudal ties. It was not easy to keep society going when so many people died so quickly. Strong rulers helped to keep order, and that helped to strengthen kings and city governments.

By about 1500, Europe was changing. Both kings and towns were stronger. Knights and armor were on the way out; cannon and cannon balls were on the way in. Kings and city governments both founded more universities so that more people could study law, medicine, and other subjects. In Italy, learned people had begun to look back to the learning and the art produced by ancient Greeks and Romans thousands of years before them. The movement we call the Renaissance had begun. There were more cities and more trade. Some traders began to look for more ways to trade with more people outside of Europe, going as far as Africa and even to America. With the dawn of these new times, the Middle Ages—the world of feudalism, lords and vassals, serfs, knights, and courtly love—faded into the past.

abbot the leader of a monastery

charter a document given by a government or ruler to a group of people or a company

circuit an area or district through which a judge travels to hold court sessions

Code of Chivalry a set of rules for knights

convent a community of women who devote themselves to religious life

cooper a person who makes barrels

dauphin the title given to the eldest son of the king of France

excommunication the punishment of not allowing someone to continue as a member of the Church

feudalism a system of government in which land is exchanged for loyalty and services

fief a plot of land exchanged for loyalty to a ruler

journeyman an apprentice who is qualified to work in a particular trade

jury a group of people who hear evidence in a trial and then vote on the guilt or innocence of the accused

knight a military servant of a feudal king or other superior

manor the estate over which a lord had control; also the lord's house on an estate

monastery a community of monks

pilgrimage a journey undertaken for a religious purpose

plague a highly contagious, usually fatal, disease that affects large numbers of people

serf a farmworker who was bound to live and labor on his lord's land

smith a person who works with metals, such as a goldsmith, silversmith, tinsmith, or blacksmith

tournament a staged battle fought by knights for money and honor without the intention to wound or kill

troubadour a person who composed poems that were set to music

truce an agreement to stop fighting

vassal a person who receives land from a ruler and in return promises aid

CREDITS